Down Home Delicious

Spice up your Life with Incredible Gulf Coast Cooking

by Peggy Touchtone Sholly

Stonywood Publications
P.O. Box 1590
Pearland, Texas 77581
800-335-1280
www.stonywood.com

Down Home Delicious

Spice up your life with incredible Gulf Coast cooking

ORIGINAL SPECIAL REQUEST RECIPES

Distinctly American Favorites,
Irresistibly Italian American,
Deep in the Heart of TexMex,
Lip Smackin' Louisiana and
"I love you this much" Desserts

Peggy Touchtone Sholly

A private collection of original and favorite recipes
Published by Stonywood Publications

includes
Lagniappe by Kimberly Fay and Robert Sholly

Down Home Delicious
Spice up your life with incredible Gulf Coast cooking
by Peggy Touchtone Sholly

Edited, designed and published by
Stonywood Publications
P.O. Box 1590
Pearland, Texas 77581
www.stonywood.com

Manufactured by Favorite Recipes Press
An imprint of FRP
P.O. Box 305142
Nashville, Tennessee 37230
800-358-0560

Cover layout: C. Stevenson
Art: Jay Mazhar, Illustrator
Makeup Artist: Andrea Shutter
Photographer: Brian Edison

First Printing 2007
10,000 Copies

Publisher's Cataloging-in-Publication
(Provided by Quality Books, Inc.)

Sholly, Peggy Touchtone
    Down home delicious : spice up your life with incredible Gulf Coast cooking /
by Peggy Touchtone Sholly. -- 1st ed.
    p. cm.
    Includes index.
    LCCN 2007904670.
    ISBN-13: 978-0-9796652-0-2
    ISBN-10: 0-9796652-0-5

    1. Cookery, American.   I. Title.

TX715.S46 2008   641.5973
                     QBI07-700134

Printed in China

Dedication

I dedicate this book to:

- My adorable husband, the surprise love of my life, who brings me happiness in marriage that I never knew before. He has been my inspiration to write and publish this book.

- My children, Jay Housholder, Kimberly Fay, and Keith Housholder, who have been the loves of my life since the day of their conception and always will be. They have always affirmed my cooking so highly that it has been a great foundation for my courage to step out in this endeavor.

- My grandchildren who are so beautiful, precious and innocent and I love them all with all my heart.

Foreword

-----Down Home Delicious-----

Peggy Sholly and Chef Randy Evans

As a chef of a fine dining restaurant everyone asks me where I eat and what I enjoy eating. My answer is that most of the time I eat what I grew up eating. Homemade stews, fresh vegetables, cookies, and cakes are still what I enjoy and *Down Home Delicious* offers just that. Peggy takes you through a journey of her culinary upbringing from Louisiana as a child and young adult to Texas as a mother feeding her loving family.

This cookbook is a guide for those not comfortable cooking from scratch and who might need a little direction in the kitchen. The recipes offer detailed instructions that are easy to follow and recreate and which have been tested with great success by amateur cooks with little experience in the kitchen. As a teenager learning how to cook from my mother, the hardest part was to repeat the dish successfully without a recipe. This book takes the guess work out of the kitchen and allows the cook to be confident that every recipe will be the same - every attempt. When cooking for family or friends there is no need to worry if the dish will taste as good as it did the first time. These recipes are straight forward and easily prepared.

Down Home Delicious is a great book for those just attempting to cook for the first time or for the seasoned cook. I love the variety it offers from Peggy's Italian heritage to good ole Tex-Mex with a good amount of Louisiana mixed in. Its recipes are written from the soul and have character to them. Food is about the soul and *Down Home Delicious* is certainly soulful.

Chef Randy Evans
Brennan's of Houston
The Kitchen Table

Down Home Delicious

Spice up your life with incredible Gulf Coast cooking

Contents

About the Author

I am not a chef, but I am a great everyday cook. I almost had to be, from my earliest childhood in Baton Rouge, Louisiana I was continually exposed to a cornucopia of flavors and spices and incredibly delicious foods.

Many people paint, or write, or whittle things. I cook and I love it! Cooking is my passion after my husband and children. I have always felt like there was something more I needed to do but couldn't put my finger on it. There was this emptiness that needed filling even though I led a very busy life. Now I know that writing this book is the destiny I had not yet identified and I have derived much satisfaction in preparing it for your use.

Cooking has many faces and places in my life. Some days cooking provides a healing touch; in my kitchen that includes varieties of homemade chicken soup, lasagna, or oatmeal cookies. At times, cooking is therapeutic; chopping, stirring, and blending whatever is in the pantry and refrigerator, it releases pent-up emotions in a productive manner, the process and product soothing the wounded soul. When I am bored I work on creating a new recipe or a new version of an old one. Always satisfying, cooking takes me back to my roots as I make a large pot of Suga (slow cooked Italian tomato gravy). Or throw together an Ultimate Chocolate Indulgence cake or chocolate dipped strawberries to delight my husband. If I'm really in "the zone" I may prepare a dish of lasagna for neighbors or guests, or cook "special request" jambalaya or etouffee.

Some of my most precious childhood memories are of my grandmother serving simple, steaming platters of pasta to my Aunts, Uncles and the children. She made beautiful loaves of Italian bread from scratch, without a recipe, and baked marvelous, memory making Italian goodies like biscotti and Italian fig cookies by the hundreds. I was fortunate to get the fig cookie and biscotti recipes which I have shared in this book. I didn't really realize at the time what an impact the food customs in my life were having on me.

As a child in an Italian American family, meals were social events, and cooking a source of joy and pride. I enjoyed a wide variety of Italian American foods, simple and delicious. Good memories abound of those meals shared in my grandparents home over heaping plates of slow cooked suga and pasta with meatballs, a Sunday regular. Growing up in this environment contributed to the nurturing of my personal creative streak and was the foundation for my experimentation and development of recipes.

At age 11, my love affair with food and a flair for developing my own recipes began. Because I had no recipes to follow, I saw cooking as a creative outlet to gift others through the work of my hands. It was a source of satisfaction and joy for me as it was for others and greatly contributed to my feelings of self worth. My first culinary creation, an humble beginning, was a no-recipe homemade vegetable soup. Along with fresh vegetables available in our refrigerator, it included dried prunes and a pillaged ear of corn from my neighbor's garden. A visiting uncle was the proud recipient of this first effort and he graciously ate it with great gusto. I still remember his joyful laughing. At the time I thought it was because I had prepared the dish especially for him. Now I think it was probably the prunes – at the time I had no idea they were inappropriate for soup.

My creative fascination with food and the confidence to develop my own recipes began with that homemade vegetable soup. But that was as far as it went at the time. Satisfied I could accomplish that feat successfully, I turned my attention to singing, sewing and school activities, where again I had much success. Like with the cooking, I taught myself to sew and made all my own clothes, mixing patterns to make new designs. The creative bent was still there, just in a different direction. I also sang at functions throughout Baton Rouge, on radio, stage, and television. I loved to ballroom dance and spent many hours dancing whenever I could. I was involved in many leadership activities and busy all the time. While attending LSU in Baton Rouge I decided to give up performing, and married.

As an adult responsible for family meals the memories floated up from my psyche and colored my food experiences and expectations. My cooking went into overdrive, the performing energy now being directed to producing delicious foods for my family and friends. As my confidence grew, I added tastes that I loved. From the beginning I never feared to jump in and try something new. Recipe didn't work? Try it again another day. As time went on, I developed my own personal cooking style, an art form that bubbles forth from my Italian heritage; an expression of love rife with creativity and tradition, now made richer by the ethnic influences of Louisiana and Texas.

My husband's job moved us from Louisiana to Texas to Michigan to Kentucky to California. Eventually we settled in Texas where I have lived for the past 30 years. During my adult life on the flavor trail, from New Orleans to West Texas, peppered with jaunts to California and Europe, I journeyed from housewife and cook, to mother, business woman, and now author. I experienced friendships with phenomenal cooks and chefs that added richly to my life and my love of food and its preparation. I am grateful to all these wonderful individuals.

I enjoyed much success to the detriment of my husband's waistline while my love of cooking bloomed. Over the years my recipes have been taste tested across the country with rave reviews as I entertained family, friends and business associates. Many requested I share my private recipes or teach them to cook.

As I mentioned, I began my culinary journey in Baton Rouge, where families and friends bond during meals and various celebrations. Most everyone I knew was a cook-without-recipes cook and all were comfortable adding their own personal touch to recipes. At home we indulged ourselves with pasta in many forms, plus fresh fried fish, hush puppies, tartar sauce, seafood etouffee, gumbo, Jambalaya, boiled crayfish and much more. As an adult in Texas, TexMex favorites like enchiladas, salsa, guacamole, Mexican rice, Caldo de Res and others were added to our table.

To my knowledge, no one in my family owned a cookbook and there was seldom a spoiled dish or bland meal. The secret? The same secret that produced culinary legends like Emeril Lagasse, Paul Prudhomme, and Justin Wilson… it's what we do in Louisiana and on the coast of Texas. We cook and feed people. Life in Louisiana revolves around food, not just good food but Great food everyday, every meal. Everyone cooks in Louisiana, men, women and children. My Dad taught my Mom to cook basic American classics like cornbread and biscuits, stew, greens, and more. We boil, stir, fry or barbeque everything from gumbo to fried catfish fresh from the stream, river or lake and prepare fried chicken accompanied by cast iron pots of steaming hot red beans and steamed rice. We cook what we like with the ingredients we like and sure enough, we eventually master it and the food is as good as it comes. One lesson I learned early on, fast is not always best. The best flavors often take a little longer. Don't shorten the time, steps, or seasonings if you want a truly delicious dish.

I have also learned that when it comes to romance, a delicious meal well prepared, can establish a romantic environment. Throughout the ages man has wined and dined his prospective love interest and she, him. My personal experience has proved the old saying "The way to a man's heart is through his stomach." I must admit I have used my cooking talent to dine the socks off my husband. When he walks in the door and smells the wonderful aromas of his favorite foods wafting through the house his eyes begin to sparkle. He full well knows I'm romancing him and loves every moment of it. My children also respond to the scent of their favorites. They recognize the love it conveys and it makes them feel special. With my efforts being so well received, I get many hugs and kisses and continue to scout for new favorites and great tastes I can add to my collection.

Although my voice is no longer entertaining, I still love to dance, garden, and travel in addition to cooking. I am family centered and very happily married to the man who continued to push me to make this book a reality. Cooking is still a passion of mine and I believe always will be.

In my life, the sharing of good food lovingly prepared creates a memory thread of good times that connects one person to another. It fuels romance, bonds families, strengthens friendships, invites others into my family circle, and satisfies the soul. Thank y'all for becoming a part of my extended family as you share my recipes with your family and friends.

Acknowledgements
-----*Down Home Delicious*-----

From the conception of this book I have been blessed with constant support, encouragement and assistance from my much loved husband, Bob. In his inevitably gentle way he pushed, prodded, researched and wrote, edited and critiqued, financed and marketed, and assured me that there is, within the grand scheme of things, an important reason for sharing my gift with others within and without our family. He has been my compass during this tedious yet fulfilling adventure. Along the way many others have also come forward to help and encourage. In addition to being deeply indebted at all times to the devotion and love of my husband, without whom *Down Home Delicious* would never have been birthed, and even when the stress was picking away at me, I am also indebted to certain family and friends.

First of all there is my darling daughter who put hundreds of hours into testing and critiquing recipes, putting the recipes in Adobe Creative Suite for printing, and all this in the midst of a difficult pregnancy followed by a new love of my life, Baby Francesca Fay, and working a full time job. Working on the book together has been a deep bonding experience and a joy as I observed my daughter move from someone with extremely limited cooking skills to a truly good cook. Her growth and dedication to the finished product has been exciting and heartwarming and my motherly pride overflows for having the opportunity to share this with her. Knowing how everything 'should' taste, she has personally cooked 95% of the recipes in the book and contributed her forthright comments to taste and ease of understanding and preparation of recipes. She fed the dishes to many friends and acquaintances and received rave reviews, great for keeping the ball moving.

Next there is Patrick Hammer who kindly tasted every recipe and provided significant positive and creative comments along the way.

I must also say a big THANK YOU to my friend of some 25 years, Dr. Gaye Perry, who has believed in me and supported me all the years of our acquaintance, and now affirmed, encouraged, and assisted Bob and me with the creative aspects of my cookbook. Her many talents and friendship have been a great gift throughout the many years I have known her.

I have much gratitude for the support of several long-term friends that have been by my side, for almost 30 years, offering me encouragement and support. In no particular order, there is Reta DeBottis, Alice Hopper, and Mary Voigt who believe in me and keep me going when my spirit is waning and I need revitalizing. Thank you gals. You're great friends!

I am also indebted to the staff of FRP our printer and distributor, Jay Mazhar my illustrator, and Cathi Stevenson our cover designer for all the patient assistance provided in directing my efforts on this project when I asked questions over and over and over again.

Even my step-daughter, Cheron Hill, jumped right in and helped with some of the creative writing critiques on a visit here. What more can I say, I am a fortunate woman to have such family and friends to bring my dream to fruition with me.

When we were on a short dead line for submission, Kevin Herrod stepped in and provided his extraordinary expertise on graphic design to tie up the loose ends and help make this a real book. Thank you, Kevin.

We are indebted to Chef Randy Evans, Executive Chef of Brennan's of Houston and author of *The Kitchen Table*. Chef Randy's review and foreword for this book provides a succinct and clear outline of what *Down Home Delicious* is all about. We expect Chef Randy soon to be as well-known as Emeril Legasse who established his reputation at another Brennan's restaurant, the Commander's Palace in New Orleans.

I have heard it takes a village to raise a child. Believe me, it has taken a village to birth *Down Home Delicious* and we all share in the joy of its finally being in print and available to the public.

Disclaimer

-----Down Home Delicious-----

The information in this book was designed, written, compiled and published as an instructional reference book. It is not meant to be totally comprehensive about cooking or anything else within this publication. This book is primarily a guide for those who love to cook and want to add new recipes to their repertoire or try new tastes. It will add unexpected surprises to the serving of meals in a fashion to entertain and bond with family and guests. If you want to be an expert cook I suggest you continue to read all you can and also try dishes published by others in order to further your skills and refine your tastes.

It is the author's desire that even beginners will be able to navigate these recipes with ease and produce tasty dishes that will please even the most finicky eaters. No one connected with *Down Home Delicious* can guarantee that everyone will be successful in the preparation of these meals considering how limited the written word is in conveying some informational skills.

Every effort has been made to make these recipes as complete and easy to understand as possible when not able to answer questions face to face.

The purpose of this book is to share the author's passion for cooking and part of her private recipe collection that have been requested by others over the years. It is her culinary legacy to family and friends throughout the world, including the new ones acquired through the publication of this work.

The author, Peggy Touchtone Sholly, Stonywood Publications, and contributor Kimberly Fay shall not have liability or responsibility to any person or entity for any alleged loss or damage caused directly or indirectly by the recipes or information contained in or connected to this publication.

If you choose not to be bound by any of the above, you may return this book to the publisher with a note as to the reason for return, accompanied by your purchase receipt for a full refund of the purchase price and cost of shipping and handling to return said book. Please contact publisher in advance of return so that you may receive an assigned return acceptance number. It is our expectation that instead of desiring to return a book our customers will be so delighted with this product they will choose to order additional copies for family and friends. Enjoy!

Introduction...

On the Flavor Trail
from New Orleans to West Texas

Introduction

Writing a book is often compared to giving birth, except the natural experience normally ends in nine months. The birth of this cookbook has taken fifty years and much like normal childbirth, a lot of it was sheer joy. The difficult parts have been softened with time and the overall result is a source of great pride.

In this age of obesity and dieting run amuck, the soul yearns for delicious satisfying foods that quench the pangs of hunger in a significant manner. Fast foods and restaurants can't compete with truly good home cooked foods because of their necessity to produce in such large quantities. In my travels throughout the country I always run across people who have originally come from Texas or Louisiana or the Gulf Coast. Invariably they comment on how much they miss the cooking of "down-home." Even folks who have never set foot along the Gulf Coast hear so much about southern, "Coast" or TexMex cooking they think they would like, but it is not available in their area or it is not comparable to the home cooked flavor the Louisiana and Texas natives enjoy. *Down Home Delicious* endeavors to make these wonderful, satisfying flavors available in your own kitchen with easy to follow instructions fit for anyone from novice to expert. Now, wherever you may be, you can prepare a good hot chili, spicy soup, fried chicken, fried fish and pasta, tacos, salsas, smothered hamburger steak and chicken and dumplings to rival the best on the Gulf Coast without worrying about transfat issues or salt in fast food take out.

Down Home Delicious gathers up some of the old recipes for meals that have been in families for generations plus many newer, more current original version recipes and provides them in a fresh manner. They are for cooks just starting out or for cooks who are looking for recipes that are tested and true and who can't quite forget the meals that Grandma fixed on Sundays for the whole family. Many of these dishes are recognized in Louisiana and Texas as regular fare, but they won't be found in non-specialty cookbooks.

In the beginning, …when my sons got married, their new wives didn't know how to cook, particularly Italian, Louisiana and Texas style. This was a problem because my sons always made comparisons between their wife's cooking and Mom's cooking. I understand this is not an uncommon thing, but my sons were both good cooks and expected their wives to cook at least as well as themselves. Little by little the young women began asking me how I fixed certain beloved dishes. Since I was a "cook-without-recipes" cook, I had to start measuring out amounts, writing down the recipes, and putting them into my computer in order to share the recipes with my daughters-in-law. It certainly was easier to better understand a recipe rather than "take a couple of pinches of this and about a half cup of that and mix them together with two handfuls of the rest of it."

I got into the habit of putting my recipes into my computer as I cooked them. My collection grew and affirmation for my cooking abounded. Family members, friends, and guests praised and made special requests for many of my recipes and sought advice on how to cook all manner of foods. I included all of these favored foods into my burgeoning file. My husband insisted I put my collection into book form as a family legacy. I had often said I had at least one book in me. I meant a book of fiction –the possibility of a cookbook never crossed my mind. As my recipe collection grew I was constantly told that the work in progress needed to be shared with the public as well as the family. Support has been enormous. Everyone who heard about what I was doing wanted a personal copy of the book and so strongly did they believe others would also enjoy my private collection, they wanted additional copies to give as gifts. With all that positive response I agreed to have the book published for the public. *Down Home Delicious* is the result.

When we got serious about going to press, I made every effort to design the cookbook in such a manner that the recipes are easy enough for a beginner and still delicious and tempting enough for the seasoned cook.

Distinctly American Favorites run the gamut from meatloaf, chicken and dumplings, roast beef and roast chicken, and turkey cooked the old fashioned way. Vegetables are sautéed, fried, stewed, roasted and baked. Mmmmm, mmmmm, good! There are soups and salads that will bring back wonderful memories and are robust meals or light side dishes for larger entrees.

The Irresistibly Italian American section gives you original Italian meat sauce, meatballs, lasagna, pasta and roasted vegetables, all with a distinctly Louisiana flair. Lip Smackin' Louisiana provides you a spread of French, Cajun and Creole dishes that are the core of

Louisiana cookery. Fish, seafood, shrimp, crawfish, potatoes, corn, gumbo, jambalaya, beans and potato salad are all representative of the entries in this section.

In TexMex you will be pleased to note that now you can even learn how to make some real chili, enchiladas, tacos, tamales, beans, guacamole and several kinds of salsa and pico de gallo. You can even find tips on how Texans select, buy and grill the perfect steak!

I Love you This Much - Just Desserts has some basic great desserts like my grandmother's Italian Biscotti and her Fig Cookies as well as some of my original creations like Sweet Tater 'Umpkin Pie and White Chocolate Nuts and Bolts. My version of Ultimate Chocolate Indulgence, at least according to my husband, is the most delicious chocolate cake ever to come out of an oven. I don't know if that is true, but it is always nice to hear.

In addition to all these great foods, there are sprinkles of entertainment and hospitality tips throughout the book and the Lagniappe (lan-yap) portion provides a little something extra with notes on the history and origins of various types of food and ingredients.

For those of you still wishing for that "down-home" flavor, here you are; I expect the recipes will be a source of enjoyment and pleasure for all who prepare these authentic down-home dishes. For those who haven't tried these Louisiana and Texas Gulf Coast historical and cultural prize winners…prepare yourself for a flavor trail treat!

Distinctly American Favorites

Loving you is the best thing I do...

Contents

-----Distinctly American Favorites-----

Beef Hash

-----Distinctly American Favorites-----

In my family, we look forward to roast in anticipation of the hash that follows. This is a great way to use that leftover roast when you are tired of sandwiches.

SERVES 4

3	tablespoons vegetable oil
1	medium onion, chopped
½-1	pound sliced mushrooms
1-2	tablespoons garlic
-	drippings or gravy from roast
4	cups boiling water, chicken or beef broth
1	bay leaf, optional Kosher salt and ground black pepper, to taste
2-4	cups leftover beef roast with fat removed, cut in 1" cubes
3	large red potatoes, peeled and cubed similar to beef

Heat a 4-quart pot with oil until hot but not smoking. Add onions and mushrooms and sauté until onions begin to soften. Add garlic and sauté for an additional minute, stirring constantly. Add drippings, water, and bay leaf, and bring to a gentle boil. Add salt and pepper, adjusting seasonings as necessary.

Add roast cubes meat and bring all back to a low boil. Cover pot with a lid and simmer over low heat until meat is tender, time will be determined by the cut of beef. If using bay leaf, remove now.

Add cubed potatoes, bring back to a low boil, and cook 15 minutes or just until fork tender. (Suggestion: Remove meat from juice temporarily while you cook potatoes in liquid, then return meat when potatoes are tender and seasoned properly. Its easier to adjust salt for potatoes without over salting the meat. In additional, potatoes tend to sap flavor from other items.)

Serve with homemade corn bread.

Garlicky Pan-Seared Steak

-----Distinctly American Favorites-----

When using a meat thermometer, be sure to insert the rod into the center of the thickest part of the flesh.

SERVES 2-4

2	1½-inch thick (12 ounce each) Angus boneless rib eye or other high quality steaks
2	tablespoons olive oil flavored with 1 teaspoon minced garlic
1	teaspoon coarse ground black pepper
1	teaspoon Kosher salt
2	tablespoons room temperature butter

Preheat oven to 250 degrees.

Pat steaks dry and allow to sit at room temperature for 15 to 20 minutes. While steaks are sitting, put olive oil and 1 teaspoon minced garlic in a small glass bowl and microwave 1 minute, and then set aside. Turn oven to 200 degrees and put empty platter in oven to warm.

Sprinkle both sides of each steak with pepper.

Strain oil into large skillet and heat, over moderately high heat, until hot but not smoking. Sauté seasoned steaks, on medium high heat turning over once midway through, 10 to 12 minutes for medium rare, and 12-14 minutes for medium.

Put steaks on warm platter, sprinkle salt over both, top with butter, and allow to rest, covered with foil, for about 5 minutes. Either cut steaks in half and serve four, or serve one steak each to 2 individuals, or slice steaks across grain in 1-inch strips and serve.

Steak is great served with Simple Italian Salad or Warm TexMex Corn Salad piled on top.

Beef Lettuce Wraps

-----Distinctly American Favorites-----

A great change of pace meal that is fun for all and definitely delicious. A great little appetizer.

SERVES 6

8	large mushrooms
2	green onions minced
2	cloves garlic minced
1	(8-ounce) can water chestnuts, chopped
	iceberg or butter lettuce "cup" leaves
1	package cellophane Chinese rice noodles
5	tablespoons cooking oil

Cooking Sauce

¼	teaspoon beef granules
½	teaspoon ground ginger
1	tablespoon Soy sauce
1	teaspoon sherry, optional
3	tablespoons water or pineapple juice
1	tablespoon cooking oil
1	teaspoon brown sugar
2	teaspoons cornstarch

Marinade Sauce

1	teaspoon cornstarch
1	tablespoon water or pineapple juice
¼	teaspoon each salt and pepper
½	of the garlic (1 clove fresh garlic, minced)
½	of the green onion (1 green onion, minced)
1	tablespoon Soy sauce
¼	teaspoon ground red chili pepper
1	teaspoon sesame or other cooking oil
1½	pounds boneless, Angus steak, fat removed, or 1 ½ pounds Angus ground sirloin (it is easier if you purchase the meat already ground)

Sauce for Wraps

2	tablespoons brown sugar
3	tablespoons Soy sauce
1	teaspoon red chili hot sauce, (Optional)

Cut mushrooms and discard stems. Mince mushroom caps and set aside. Mince onions and garlic and set aside. Use half of onions and garlic for marinade and half for cooking. Chop water chestnuts and set aside. Separate lettuce leaves and gently rinse and pat fry. Prepare noodles according to package directions.

Break drained and cooked cellophane noodles into small pieces, and cover bottom of serving dish with them. Set aside.

Cooking Sauce – Mix all cooking sauce ingredients in bowl and set aside.

Marinade Sauce – In medium bowl, combine cornstarch, water (or pineapple juice), salt and pepper, garlic, green onions, Soy sauce and ground red chili pepper. Stir well, then let sit while you prepare beef.

If meat is not already ground, put beef in processor and pulse until ground, or slice into very small squares. Add beef to marinade bowl. Stir to coat beef thoroughly, stir in marinade oil and let sit 15 minutes to marinate.

Cooking – Put wok or large skillet over medium high heat and add 3 tablespoons oil. Add beef and stir fry for about 3-4 minutes. Remove beef and set aside.

Add 2 tablespoons oil to skillet. Add 1 teaspoon each of remaining garlic and onion; stir fry about a minute.

Add mushrooms and stir fry an additional 2 minutes.

Return beef to pan. Add mixed cooking sauce to pan along with water chestnuts. Cook until thickened and hot. (Drain meat in colander only if you prefer less fat.)

Pour cooked beef mixture on top of noodles in serving dish. Let guests spoon mixture into individual lettuce leaves, top with a little sauce for wraps, roll leaf and eat.

To round off the meal you may choose to serve these with stir fried or grilled vegetables of choice.

Beef Roast with Vegetables

-----Distinctly American Favorites-----

Warm and hearty, satisfies even the manliest man. Add vegetables of your choice including chopped bell peppers, green cabbage, artichoke quarters or bottoms, carrots and frozen green peas.

SERVES 6-8

2	**(14-ounce) cans beef stock water**
1	**large onion, minced**
1	**tablespoon minced garlic**
1	**bay leaf**
1	**(8-ounce) can tomato sauce, optional**
1	**teaspoon salt**
1	**teaspoon coarse ground pepper**
3-4	**pounds good quality chuck, round, or sirloin tip roast**
1	**cup seasoned flour (seasoned with salt, pepper and garlic powder)**
	vegetable oil
8	**ounces sliced mushrooms**
½-1	**cup each of 2-3 additional vegetables, optional**

Put a couple inches water or beef stock (or a combination of the two) into a large pot sprayed with cooking spray. Add onions, garlic, bay leaf, tomato sauce (optional), salt and pepper and bring to a gentle boil.

Season roast either whole or cut in large chunks then coat lightly with seasoned flour. If you do not like gravy made with flour, omit flour step and proceed as follows. Spray or coat a large skillet, pour in about ½ inch of vegetable oil and heat over high heat. Brown meat quickly on all sides. Remove meat from skillet and add it to the hot stock.

Bring stock back up to a boil, cover pot with a lid, and immediately reduce heat to simmer. Simmer a couple of hours or until meat is barely tender when checked with a fork (length of time depends on cut and quality of meat – Angus is the most tender in the least amount of time). When tender, remove bay leaf.

Add mushrooms, and 2-3 optional vegetables of choice to gravy. Continue cooking until all vegetables are barely tender. Adjust seasonings and serve with mashed potatoes, rice or hot corn bread.

Deluxe Prime Rib

-----Distinctly American Favorites-----

Elegant and luscious. Serve with sauteed mushrooms, asparagus, roasted small red potatoes or flavored rice.

SERVES 6

3-4   **pound Angus Prime Rib, well marbled with bone**

2   **tablespoons finely minced fresh garlic, enough pepper to season lightly salt**

<u>Total Roasting Time per pound</u>
Rare
22 minutes per pound

Medium
26 minutes per pound

Well-done
31 minutes per pound

Rather than seasoning with store bought marinades, you can make your own rub with garlic powder and cracked black peppercorns.

Preheat oven to 500 degrees. Pat or sprinkle seasonings over entire roast then spray whole roast lightly with cooking spray. Or make a rub of one tablespoon garlic powder and up to 3 tablespoons cracked black peppercorns (depending on how much pepper you like). Put roast, rib side down, on a rack in a pan sprayed with cooking oil.

Bake at 500 degrees for 10 minutes. Put a small foil tent, sprayed underneath with cooking spray, on top of the roast if it gets too dark on the top. Reduce temperature to 400 degrees and bake an additional 25-30 minutes per pound or to desired degree of doneness (at this point, use a meat thermometer to test – remember, roast will continue to cook when out of the oven so cook to medium if you want medium well).

Remove roast from pan and place on serving plate. Let the meat sit 15 minutes before slicing.

Surround base of roast with sautéed mushrooms and/or artichoke bottoms, or whatever you prefer. When using artichoke bottoms, be sure to rinse and gently scrape out feather-like part.

Reserve drippings and de-glazing from pan to be used for gravy. Adjust seasonings as necessary. Heat thoroughly.

Meatloaf

-----Distinctly American Favorites-----

This is so good you may want to double the recipe so you can make sandwiches with leftovers or use for hamburgers.

SERVES 4-6

2	**pounds ground chuck (or 1 pound each ground chuck and pork)**
¾	**cup plain bread crumbs**
1	**tablespoon dry onion flakes**
1	**tablespoon beef granules**
½	**teaspoon dry flakes or 1 teaspoon fresh minced, parsley**
1	**tablespoon fresh minced garlic**
½	**cup water**
2	**jumbo or 3 small eggs, lightly beaten**
¾	**teaspoon salt**
1	**teaspoon pepper**
4	**ounces water, or chicken or beef stock**
8	**ounces seasoned tomato sauce**
½	**cup water, or chicken or beef broth**
	rings of green pepper or onion for top, optional

Mix all ingredients, except tomato sauce and the ½ cup of water, by hand until well blended. Form into 2 loaves and place in baking pan greased, sprayed with oil. Do not permit meat to touch the sides of the pan. Leave a small gutter around loaf.

If using rings, place on top of meatloaf. Sprinkle with additional onion flakes, pour tomato sauce, add ½ cup water or broth in bottom of container, then lightly season loaves with salt and pepper. To be sure of your seasonings prior to cooking, take a small amount of uncooked meat mixture and fry it like a hamburger. Taste and adjust seasonings accordingly. Just don't succumb to frying and eating it all right then. Meatloaf may be wrapped in foil and frozen for cooking at a later date.

When ready to cook, bake at 375 degrees for 1¼ to 1½ hours, basting after first 30 minutes if top becomes very dry.

Allow to cool for at least 10 minutes before serving. Use drippings for gravy. Leftovers make delicious sandwiches.

Mouth Waterin' Meatloaf

-----Distinctly American Favorites-----

This is definitely the tastiest meatloaf anywhere, juicy and bursting with flavor yet fast and simple to make. It can be mixed and shaped earlier in the day, wrapped tightly in plastic wrap and refrigerated or frozen until ready to cook.

SERVES 4-6

1	**pound ground chuck**
1	**pound fresh ground pan sausage or pack Owens, Jimmie Dean, etc. in a roll**
1	**(3-ounce) can French's Fried onions**
½	**cup oatmeal mixed with ¼ cup water to soften**
1	**tablespoon beef granules**
1	**teaspoon each salt and pepper**
¼	**teaspoon turmeric**
½	**teaspoon dry flakes or 1 teaspoon fresh minced, parsley**
1	**tablespoon fresh minced garlic**
½	**cup water**
2	**jumbo or 3 small eggs, lightly beaten**
4	**ounces water, or chicken or beef stock**
8	**ounces tomato sauce or puree**
1	**cup water**
	rings of green pepper or onion for top, optional

Put ground meat, sausage and fried onions in a 4-quart mixing bowl. In another bowl, mix oatmeal, beef granules, salt, pepper, turmeric, parsley, garlic and ½ cup water and set aside for oatmeal to soften. Beat eggs in a small bowl.

Preheat oven to 375 degrees. Spray a bread loaf pan lightly with oil or grease. Add eggs to meat and onion bowl and use your hands (plastic gloves are good here) to mix meat, onion and eggs together. Add bowl with oatmeal seasonings to meat bowl and mix well into meat mixture. When well mixed, transfer all into loaf pan. Use straightened fingers to push between sides of meat loaf and pan, making a gutter all around. Pour ½ the water or stock into the gutter.

If using rings, place on top of meatloaf. Pour tomato sauce over top of meatloaf. Then lightly sprinkle loaf with salt and pepper.

Bake for 1¼ to 1½ hours, adding additional water as needed to keep gutter moist or if top becomes very dry.

Allow to cool for at least 10 minutes before serving. Leftovers make delicious sandwiches.

Perfect Beef Pot Roast

-----Distinctly American Favorites-----

Serve this with steamed rice and crusty bread or corn bread and watch your diner's delight. The flavors and texture combinations make your tastebuds sing.

SERVES 4

4	**cups water or meat broth**
2-3	**pounds chuck or top sirloin beef roast**
	garlic powder
	Kosher salt
	black pepper
¼	**cup all purpose flour seasoned with salt and pepper, optional**
4	**tablespoons vegetable oil**
1	**teaspoon Kosher salt**
½	**teaspoon black pepper**
1	**large yellow onion, cut in chunks**
1-2	**tablespoons chopped garlic**
1	**(8-ounce) can diced tomatoes, optional**
4-6	**cups total assorted vegetables of your choice**

You can vary your favorite ingredients by adding the vegetables you love such as mushrooms, carrots, red potatoes, celery, bell pepper, and frozen peas.

Spray a 4-quart or larger pot with oil. Add 4 cups water or broth and bring to a boil.

Cut meat into very large pieces, then lightly season meat on all sides with garlic powder (not salt), salt, and pepper. If you prefer thicker gravy, dust meat with seasoned flour.

While liquid is coming to a boil. Add vegetable oil to a large skillet and bring to high heat; quickly brown meat on all sides. Transfer meat to boiling liquid; add salt and pepper and bring to a gentle boil. Add onions to meat skillet and sauté. When tender, add sautéed onions and chopped garlic to roast. You may add a small can diced tomatoes at this time. Be sure meat is simmering before covering pot with tight fitting lid. Simmer meat over low heat at least one hour, or until fork tender. Some meats may require a longer cooking time. Adjust seasonings. After cooking, cool and remove fat and bring back to a boil.

Add vegetables to pot and bring to a boil. Turn heat to low, place lid back on pot, and cook for 20 minutes, or until potatoes are tender. Adjust seasonings.

Simple and Succulent Roast Beef

-----*Distinctly American Favorites*-----

It doesn't get much better than this. Hot and juicy with gravy from the drippings. Yum! Tenderness of roast will depend on quality of meat you use, therefore Angus, or comparable, is best.

SERVES ½ -pound per person
> **Angus beef roast, rump or rib eye, well marbled, 3 lbs or larger**
>
> **garlic powder (not garlic salt)**
>
> **coarse ground black pepper**
>
> **Kosher salt**

Put oven rack to middle position, then preheat oven to 450 degrees. Place meat rack into an 11 x 13-inch pan and spray both with oil.

Temperature of Cooked Meat
Rare…………..140 degrees
Medium……….150 degrees
Well-done……..170 degrees

Total cooking time according to weight:
Rare - 18 minutes per pound
Medium - 22 minutes per pound
Well-done - 25 minutes per pound

Dust all sides of roast with garlic powder, pepper and salt. Spray whole roast with cooking spray or other oil. Optional method is to pour oil in your hands and liberally apply to meat then sprinkle salt/pepper/garlic mixture over all sides.

Place meat in pan and roast, uncovered, for 30 minutes. Without opening oven door, turn heat to 400 degrees. To check doneness, insert meat thermometer into thickest part of roast; roast will continue to cook after it is removed from oven, therefore, if you want roast medium, cook it between rare and medium, (145 degrees).

Allow roast to sit for 20 minutes before serving. Remove roast to serving platter and pour drippings into a small pot. Add ½ cup water to pan and scrape up all crusty pieces and juices. Add to pot. Allow liquid to sit for several minutes then skim grease off top as much as possible. Adjust seasonings. If too strong, add more water. This is a natural gravy and therefore very thin. Heat to a simmer and serve.

Cut leftover roast into small cubes. Freeze cubes and remaining gravy (separately) to use when making hash or stew.

Vegetable Beef Stew

-----Distinctly American Favorites-----

If you want warm and comforting, this is for you! Great anytime, but particularly in cooler weather! Delicious as is or served with homemade cornbread or steamed brown rice.

SERVES 4

4	cups beef or chicken broth, or hot water
1	bay leaf, optional
2	pounds high quality beef stew meat, or chuck roast cut in cubes
	kosher salt, ground black pepper, and garlic powder
1½	cups seasoned flour
6	tablespoons vegetable oil
1	large onion, chopped chunky
2	tablespoons garlic, minced

Assorted vegetables --

1	cup each frozen green peas, optional and/or
1	cup baby or sliced carrots
2	stalks celery, washed and cut in 1 inch pieces
8	ounces sliced mushrooms
2	large red potatoes, peeled and cut in 1 inch cubes or larger
1	bell pepper, cleaned and chopped in large pieces

Spray a 4-quart or larger pot with oil, add broth or hot water and bay leaf and bring to a boil over high heat. Turn down to medium.

Sprinkle meat with garlic powder, salt and pepper, and then coat with flour. In a large skillet that has been sprayed with oil, heat 6 tablespoons oil until hot but not smoking. Add meat and lightly brown on all sides. Remove meat and put in pot of hot liquid.

In same hot skillet used for meat, sprinkle 3 tablespoons of the seasoned flour over oil and fry, stirring constantly, until brown. Turn heat to medium, add onions, and sauté until they begin to soften, stirring frequently. Add garlic and sauté for an additional minute, stirring constantly. Pour all into stew pot and bring liquid up to a gentle boil. Add salt and pepper, adjusting seasonings if necessary. Cover pot again, reduce heat to low, and cook one hour or more, until meat is tender (time depends on grade of meat).

When meat is tender, remove bay leaf. Turn heat to high, add frozen peas and bring liquid back to boil. Stir in remaining 4-6 cups vegetables, taste and adjust seasonings. Add liquid if necessary (you want to have enough liquid to generously cover all the vegetables). Bring liquid to boil again, cover pot and turn heat down to low. Cook 10-15 minutes or until potatoes are fork tender – potatoes will continue to cook after heat is off if allowed to sit in hot liquid. This can be made early in the day to allow flavors to blend and to allow fat to rise to top so it can be skimmed off.

Making Meals Meaningful - *Meals aren't only about the food on the table. The setting, atmosphere, stories, and conversations that accompany food all contribute to making even the most ordinary meal memorable. Don't forget that fun and memorable family meals can include breakfast, picnics, and meals shared with extended family and friends. Family meals are a great place to teach proper dining etiquette in a fun setting. It is important the setting is not in a forced atmosphere. This is not to be a chore but a fun time with family. There are many ideas, tucked among the recipes, to consider if mealtime at your home has become more of a chore than one of life's simple pleasures.*

Smothered Hamburger Steak

-----Distinctly American Favorites-----

Simple and satisfying. This is a continual favorite. You won't want to stop eating. Hint: When handling raw meat, wear disposable gloves to keep the bacteria from spreading in your kitchen.

SERVES 2-3

1	**pound ground sirloin, chuck or round (not too lean)**
1	**large egg, slightly beaten**
½	**teaspoon garlic powder**
1	**teaspoon salt**
1	**teaspoon ground black or white pepper**
1	**medium to large onion, sliced**
1-2	**cloves garlic or ½ teaspoon garlic powder**
3	**tablespoons extra virgin olive or other cooking oil**
2	**tablespoons butter**
8	**ounces sliced mushrooms**
1	**cup warm water**
1	**teaspoon dried parsley or cilantro**

Recipe may be doubled.

Mix ground meat, egg, garlic powder, ½ each teaspoon salt and pepper into a large bowl. Use your hands (with gloves) to mix meat and seasonings until well blended. Add water one tablespoon at a time if mixture is dry. Ground meat varies in its moisture content depending upon where it is purchased. Do not overdo water or patties will be too tender. Make 3 or 4 patties and chill in the refrigerator at least 20 minutes.

While patties are chilling, peel onion, cut in half lengthwise, and slice in ¼ inch thick slices (slices will look like half a circle). If using fresh garlic, peel and smash garlic and then cut in chunks. Set both aside.

Heat oil in a large skillet over high heat; carefully place chilled patties into hot oil. Fry until browned but not crisp, turning only once (about 2 minutes on each side). When browned, place on a warm plate. Add butter to oil in skillet and sauté onions and mushrooms over high heat until lightly brown. Add water, parsley, additional garlic, and remaining salt, and pepper. Bring to a gentle boil. Push seasonings to the side and add patties, putting onions and mushrooms on top of the meat. Reduce heat to medium low. Cover and allow ingredients to simmer for up to 30 minutes.

Chicken and Dumplings

-----Distinctly American Favorites-----

Be sure those you serve aren't faking illness just to get you to fix this for them. Not only will it satisfy that deep hunger, it is also good for whatever might ail you.

SERVES 4-6

1	**3-4 pound fryer chicken, cut up; or 8 chicken pieces of your choice**
1	**(14-ounce) can chicken broth**
16	**ounces water**
2	**stalks celery cut in 1" lengths (or 1 teaspoon celery seed)**
1	**small onion, minced**
1	**tablespoon minced garlic**
½	**teaspoon dry parsley flakes or ¼ cup fresh parsley, minced**
1	**teaspoon salt**
½	**teaspoon pepper**
	optional vegetables, fresh or canned (drain canned vegetables before using);
	mushrooms
	carrots
	green peas
	whole kernel corn
	mixed veggies
	fluffy dumplings recipe (double recipe)

Put chicken in a pot and cover with broth (or combination of water and broth) with about 2 inches of liquid above chicken. Add celery (or celery seed), onion, garlic, parsley, salt and pepper. Bring to a boil over high heat, reduce heat to low, cover and boil gently for 30 minutes.

Continue to make dumplings (see Fluffy Dumplings recipe).

After chicken has cooked 30 minutes, add vegetables and bring back to slow boil. Adjust seasonings and turn heat down to low.

Drop dumplings on top of gently simmering liquid, then carefully flip them over, cover and simmer at least 15 minutes without opening the lid.

Fluffy Dumplings

-----*Distinctly American Favorites*-----

These dumplings are a treat with the Chicken and Dumplings recipes. Can also be dropped into hot beef gravy for another taste delight.

SERVES 4-6

1½	**cups plain flour**
3	**teaspoons baking powder**
¾	**teaspoon salt**
1	**level tablespoon dried parsley flakes**
½	**teaspoon pepper**
½	**teaspoon garlic powder**
¾	**cup milk**
3	**tablespoons vegetable oil**

(Double recipe for Chicken and Dumplings)

Mix dry ingredients in a large bowl.

In a large cup or small bowl, combine milk and salad oil; add to dry ingredients, stirring until just moistened.

Drop batter from tablespoon atop slowly bubbling stew or chicken stock making sure all dumplings are approximately the same size. Gently turn dumplings over once and then bring liquid back to a slow bubbling boil.

Cover tightly, and immediately reduce heat to simmer (do not lift cover); simmer 15 to 20 minutes or until done.

Stewed Chicken and Vegetables

-----Distinctly American Favorites-----

A time-honored favorite that is comfort food at its grandest. This can be made early in the day to allow flavors to blend.

SERVES 4

4	**cups chicken broth or hot water**
1	**(10-ounce) can diced tomatoes, or Rotel tomatoes**
1	**bay leaf, optional**
1	**3-4 pound whole fryer chicken cut in pieces, or 8 pieces of choice**
	garlic powder, salt and black pepper
1	**cup seasoned flour**
½	**cup vegetable oil**
1	**large onion, chopped chunky**
1	**tablespoon minced garlic**
1	**teaspoon Kosher salt**
1	**tablespoon minced fresh, or 1 teaspoon dried, parsley**
1	**teaspoon red pepper flakes**
2	**stalks celery cut in 1-inch pieces, or ½ teaspoon celery seed**
1	**cup baby or sliced carrots, or sliced yellow squash**
2	**large red potatoes, washed and cubed**
½	**medium cabbage, cut in large chunks**

Spray a 4-quart or larger pot with oil, add broth or water, tomatoes and bay leaf and bring to a boil over high heat. Turn down to medium and cover with lid.

Lightly dust chicken on all sides with garlic powder, salt and black pepper then dust lightly with flour. In a large skillet sprayed with oil, heat 3 tablespoons oil until hot but not smoking. Add chicken and brown on all sides. When browned, add chicken to pot of hot liquid.

In the same skillet used for chicken, add additional vegetable oil if necessary and sauté onions until they begin to soften. Add garlic and sauté for an additional minute, stirring constantly. Pour all into stew pot and bring liquid up to a gentle boil. Add Kosher salt, parsley and red pepper flakes and adjust seasonings as necessary. Cover pot again, reduce heat to low, and cook 40 minutes.

Remove bay leaf, taste and adjust seasonings. Add 4-6 cups vegetables in order as listed ending with cabbage, and additional warm water if necessary, for enough liquid to cover vegetables. Bring liquid to a boil again, adjust seasonings if necessary, cover pot and cook 30 minutes. Serve with steamed rice or cornbread.

Fried Chicken with Brown Gravy

-----Distinctly American Favorites-----

Dark meat (drumsticks, thighs, and back) takes longer to cook than white meat (breast and wings). Also, size makes a difference in cooking time – the larger the piece the longer to cook. Cook dark meat in one batch and white in another.

SERVES 6-8

	canola oil or vegetable oil blend for frying
4	**cloves fresh garlic, peeled and smashed**
1	**frying chicken, (8-10 pieces), skin on and all visible fat removed**
1	**quart buttermilk**
2	**cups all-purpose flour**
1	**teaspoon salt**
1½	**teaspoon ground pepper, of choice**
½	**teaspoon garlic powder your favorite chicken seasoning, optional**
¼	**cup cornstarch**

Gravy

1	**teaspoon parsley flakes**
½	**teaspoon ground pepper chicken broth**

Coat a 12-inch skillet with spray cooking oil. Sit pan on burner but <u>do not heat</u> yet. Measure 2 to 3-inches oil into skillet and add 2 cloves of the garlic to season oil.

Place chicken pieces (cut in half) in a pan or shallow bowl, add the remaining 2 cloves garlic and pour buttermilk over all. Cover container with plastic wrap and marinate one hour at room temperature.

While chicken is marinating, set up the equipment for coating the chicken. On the counter next to the burner, place an assembly line of a cookie sheet or baking pan with a mesh strainer, and a large zip lock plastic bag. In the bag, combine flour, salt, pepper and garlic powder and mix thoroughly.

When marinating is finished, remove garlic from skillet and reserve for later use; turn heat on and heat until hot but not smoking. Shake excess buttermilk off chicken and place on the large pan; sprinkle with salt and pepper (at this time, season lightly with your favorite chicken seasoning). Put the cornstarch in the mesh strainer and lightly dust each piece by shaking the strainer with the cornstarch over the chicken, turn pieces over and repeat.

Beginning with dark meat, put chicken one piece at a time in the bag or bowl and coat each piece completely. Only do as much as will fit in the skillet at one time. Heat skillet to high and put coated chicken, skin side up, in hot grease. Dark meat is fully cooked when you make a small slit along bone in thickest area and there is no longer any pink. Drippings will be clear.

Lightly brown chicken on both sides, then reduce heat to medium-low, put lid on skillet and cook about 5-6 minutes then check. If the chicken is browning too quickly, turn down heat. Check every few minutes. When the first side is a rich golden brown, turn each piece and cook until second side is also a rich, golden brown. When cooked, remove chicken from the skillet and drain on paper towels on a warm platter. Put platter in oven to stay warm. Repeat process until all of the chicken is cooked.

Gravy
When chicken has been cooked, put garlic back into oil and sauté for 2 minutes – just until tender. Pour oil off browned flour in bottom of pan and discard oil. Return pan to heat and add 1 teaspoon parsley flakes, ½ teaspoon ground pepper, and chicken broth sufficient to make a slightly thick gravy. Heat through, taste and adjust seasonings. If gravy tastes a little "floury" continue to simmer for another 5 -10 minutes. Serve gravy with chicken, rice or mashed potatoes.

Peggy's Perfect Roast Chicken

-----Distinctly American Favorites-----

The night before you roast the chicken, sprinkle skin lightly with Kosher salt. Tie legs and tuck wings. Put chicken on a rack on top of a glass plate or glass pan, and refrigerate until ready to cook, 2 to 4 hours.

SERVES 4

1	**3-4 pound chicken**
	Kosher salt
1	**small onion, cut into ¼-inch slices separated into individual rings**
2	**cloves of garlic, sliced thick**
	extra virgin olive oil
½	**teaspoon ground black or white pepper, or for zip, use jalapeno or pepperoncini**

When ready to roast, preheat oven to 450 degrees. Using a damp paper towel, wipe salt off bird, then spray inside and out with cooking spray. Spray onion and garlic with cooking spray, dust lightly with salt, and put into cavity of chicken.

Place chicken <u>breast side down</u> onto a V-rack set in a lightly greased 11 x 13-inch pan, drizzle lightly with extra virgin olive oil, and roast in oven for about 40 minutes or until golden brown on outside. Keep an eye on chicken while it roasts and if pan drippings begin to darken too much or dry out, add ¼-½ cup warm water being careful not to let liquid touch skin.

When chicken is brown, remove pan from oven and very carefully flip chicken to where the breast is now up. Drizzle olive oil lightly over the skin, and return to oven for about another 30 minutes or until leg shakes up and down easily. If pan juices begin to dry during roasting, add ½ cup water being careful that water does not touch skin. If skin begins to brown too much, spray the dull side of a piece of aluminum foil with oil and make a tent (dull side down) over the chicken.

When chicken is finished roasting, allow it to rest at least 10 minutes before carving. Remove onion and garlic from inside body cavity, and chop.

Pour pan drippings into a bowl, add onion and garlic, season with salt and pepper as necessary and heat to high. Warm and serve with chicken. If you want more sauce you can dilute this with a small amount of chicken broth or water.

Delicious with roasted red potatoes and green beans.

Read Romantic Stories to Each Other – *Make a tray of finger foods, small sandwiches and raw veggies and dips, maybe favorite cheese chunks, and sit in the twilight on the patio or in the house somewhere comfy and read romantic stories to each other. Sharing readings like this is great fun and helps bond you to each other. For children, do the same but read ghost stories or a mystery.*

Succulent Roasted Chicken

-----Distinctly American Favorites-----

Truss your chicken with unflavored, unwaxed dental floss. Using 18-inches of floss, wrap it around the legs a few times to secure the legs together. Then, just tie the floss like you would your tennis shoes.

SERVES 4-6

3½-4	**pound chicken**
¼	**cup Kosher or regular salt**
1	**teaspoon ground pepper of choice**
	garlic powder
	spray (preferably olive oil but not necessary)
1	**small onion**
1	**tablespoon minced garlic mixed with 1 teaspoon dried chopped parsley**
1½	**tablespoons olive oil**
	water

At least six hours before (and up to one day before) serving, sprinkle chicken skin with salt (do not put inside). Set chicken on a wire rack on a plate. Refrigerate uncovered for two to four hours. The salt draws moisture from the skin and makes the skin crispy when cooked.

When ready to cook, put oven rack in the lower middle of the oven and preheat oven to 450 degrees. Cross chicken legs, tie together and tuck wings under chicken. Dust outside of chicken with pepper and garlic powder. Spray all outside of chicken with vegetable oil.

Put a V-rack in a 9 x 13-inch metal roasting pan (don't use glass) and spray all with vegetable oil. Put chicken, breast side down, on the V-rack. This will keep the breast meat from drying out. With back side up, spray again with cooking oil.

Peel an onion and cut in quarters or slice chunky. Dust onion with pepper and salt and toss with garlic mixture. Spray with vegetable oil and place in body cavity of chicken.

Roast the chicken, breast side down, until the back is deep golden brown, up to one hour for a 4-pound chicken. If drippings begin to burn (beginning to turn deepest brown towards black), add ½ cup water to the pan. If back is browning too much, put an aluminum foil tent on bird, dull side down and sprayed with cooking oil until it has cooked at least one hour.

Remove chicken from oven. With a wad of paper towels in each hand (or silicone gloves), tilt chicken so that juice in body cavity pours into pan. Flip chicken so it is breast side up, without losing the onion from body cavity. Spray with vegetable oil, then drizzle olive oil over top. Add ½ cup water to the pan, return chicken to oven and roast, breast side up, until chicken is golden brown, approximately another 20-30 minutes. Remove from oven when you can either "shake" the leg easily or until an instant–read thermometer inserted in the full part of the thigh (without touching the bone) registers 175 degrees

Transfer chicken to a serving platter for at least 15 minutes before serving warm. While chicken is resting, spoon off and discard as much of the clear fat topping liquid from drippings as possible. Remove onion from body cavity and dice. Add diced onion to drippings and use mixture to make a pan sauce of your choice to serve with chicken.

Finger Food Festival of Fun - *Pile your favorite finger foods high and enjoy the mess. Have plenty of napkins or damp personal hand towels for the meal. Easy to fix and fun to eat foods include wings, fried wontons, small meatballs made from the meatloaf recipe, ribs, fried chicken pieces, fries or tater tots or Italian roasted vegetables, fresh cherry tomatoes, corn on the cob - ask the family in advance letting each person pick one item to have. Save the list for later dates also. You don't have to cook everything yourself. Load up on deli foods from the local grocery store. Make sure you provide some spicy, some sweet, some tomato dips plus ketchup and/or mustard and pickles to accompany the finger foods.*

Grilled Lamb Chops

You are sure to love these chops even if you don't ordinarily eat lamb. Choosing lamb is easy, using color as the best indicator of quality. Pick lamb that is pinker, not deep red, and tender yet firm to the touch.

SERVES 6-10

2	**cloves fresh garlic, crushed**
2	**stalks fresh rosemary - strip leaves from stem and only use leaves**
2	**tablespoons olive oil**
¼	**cup balsamic or red wine vinegar**
6–12	**lamb chops**

Preheat outdoor grill.

Blend all items except chops in a large bowl.

Coat chops with mixture and marinate in refrigerator for not more than one hour.

Remove from marinade and pat dry. Season lightly with salt and ground black pepper. Put chops on hot grill and use remaining marinade for basting.

Cook only until brown on both sides, turning once. While grilling, do not let fire flame up onto chops (searing fat ruins meat).

Nut Crusted Shrimp

-----Distinctly American Favorites-----

The best way to discard oil is to let it cool to room temperature in the pan. Once it is cooled, pour into bowl, leftover can or ziplock bag and chill until congealed. Dump into trash and your efforts will save you a call to the plumber.

SERVES 3-4

24	**large to jumbo shrimp, shelled and de-veined, with tails on**
	seafood seasoning
	salt, ground black and cayenne pepper
½	**cup seasoned flour**
2	**large or jumbo egg white**
3	**tablespoons milk**
3	**cups spiced nuts (pecans, pistachios or peanuts are best)**

Serve with tartar sauce or over chilled Spring Mix Salad Greens tossed with Fruity Vinaigrette and garnish with fruit.

Preheat oven to 450 degrees, or deep fryer to 350 degrees. Lightly dust shrimp on both sides with seafood seasoning and/or ground black pepper and put in refrigerator to remain chilled.

Mix flour with one small pinch each of salt and ground pepper, spread on plate and set aside.

Make an egg wash by whisking together egg whites, a dash of salt and seafood seasoning or ground pepper and milk in a shallow bowl.

Finely chop spiced nuts in a food processor only until you have a mixture of larger pieces and powder. Spread on a plate and set aside.

Make an assembly line with a line of shrimp, flour mixture, egg wash, ground nuts, and a cookie sheet.

Coat shrimp <u>one at a time</u> with seasoned flour, shake off excess then dip shrimp in egg wash, letting excess drip off. Firmly press shrimp on nuts, coating shrimp completely, and put on cookie sheet, being careful not to overlap.

Bake in oven for 15 minutes, or deep fry for 3-5 minutes until golden brown and drain on paper toweling. DO NOT OVERCOOK SHRIMP.

Salmon Cakes

-----Distinctly American Favorites-----

People who do not ordinarily care for salmon often love this recipe. Don't worry about pressing hard when shaping the cakes. The egg and salmon will bind when chilled.

SERVES 2

¾   **cup flaked canned salmon, drained**

⅓   **cup crushed saltine or Club crackers**

1-2   **tablespoons chopped fresh dill or 1 teaspoon dried dill**

¼   **teaspoon white or cayenne pepper**

3   **tablespoons mayonnaise (not salad dressing)**

1   **large egg**

1   **cup bread crumbs (plain or seasoned)**

    olive oil or butter

    fresh lemon slices, optional

    tartar sauce, optional

Combine all ingredients except bread crumbs and oil or butter. Divide into cakes about 2-inches in diameter. Chill in refrigerator for 30 minutes.

Place bread crumbs in a small bowl and dip each cake into the crumbs to coat lightly.

Pour ¼ inch oil in large skillet and heat to medium or medium-high heat. Cook the fish cakes on both sides until heated through and the bread crumbs are browned, about 6 minutes.

Drain thoroughly on paper towels and keep warm until serving. Garnish with fresh lemon slices and tartar sauce if desired.

Comfort food and memories – *Every family has special foods that say comfort or home to them. Make this meal as often as you can considering everyone in the family should be present if possible. One way to signal this is the comfort meal is to get a clear plastic tablecloth and put family pictures all over the table underneath the plastic. What a fun way to encourage the sharing of family stories and memories. Maybe you could even spotlight one person each time or a special day in time.*

Talking Turkey

Such an important entree as turkey needs to be approached with wisdom. Roasting a turkey is a fairly straightforward procedure if you do it often. If not, review these guidelines to provide consistency to your meals.

1. **What size turkey to purchase**
To be sure you have plenty of turkey to eat, buy ¾ pound per person; to have enough for leftovers and seconds, buy about one pound of turkey per person.

 2. **Purchasing your turkey**
Name brand turkeys are your safest choice. Often cheaper brands have a higher salt content and can be less tender. You get what you pay for, so give quality a priority over price unless the difference is significant enough to impact your food budget negatively.

3. **Buying a fresh turkey**
The USDA recommends you purchase a fresh turkey no more than two days in advance and keep it in the coldest part of your refrigerator. The flavor and texture are superior to frozen, and they are not significantly more expensive. The timing may be tricky around holidays since the store will have the turkeys in the meat area for up to several days prior to your purchase. Also, buying fresh means you have to navigate last minute shoppers and risk the store being sold out by the time you are ready to purchase your bird.

4. **Buying a frozen turkey**
Buying frozen allows you to finish shopping early before any holiday crowds. If you purchase a frozen turkey, defrosting properly is a key factor to proper cooking and juice retention. Always thaw the turkey in the refrigerator, never at room temperature, according to package directions. A good rule of thumb is to allow a full 24 hours for every five pounds of turkey (that means an 8-10 pound turkey will require 2 days, a 10-15 pound one will require 3 days, etc.).

5. **Proper equipment**
Avoid flimsy foil pans – if possible, invest in a high-quality roasting pan, preferably no more than 2½ inches deep and large enough to accommodate the size of your whole turkey. A glass or light colored roasting pan or an enamel roaster is best suited for

proper browning of bottom of turkey. You will also need a flat roasting rack that fits your pan (or a V-rack for a turkey breast), plus an easy to read dial type meat thermometer, silicone gloves or potholders, an oven thermometer to check the accuracy of the internal temperature of your oven, untreated cotton kitchen string and a good carving set.

6. Calculating roasting times
Roasting times vary from turkey to turkey depending on temperature of oven, fat content, and internal temperature of bird. Better to chance having it done early rather than late -- it will take a long time to cool off completely.

7. Avoid dry turkey
Turkey white meat is lean and is done when it reaches 170°F. The dark meat isn't thoroughly cooked until it reaches 180 to 185°F. Protect the white meat from overcooking while the dark meat finishes cooking. When the breast is golden brown, tent the breast area with a large piece of aluminum foil sprayed with cooking oil on the dull side and put over breast with dull side down. Leave the wings and the rest of the turkey, including the meat thermometer, exposed. During the last 10-15 minutes, remove the foil so the breast skin can crisp.

8. Get the temperature right
Don't trust the pop-up timer; they are fickle and not always accurate. To properly monitor the temperature while cooking, insert a meat thermometer in the thickest part of the thigh (not touching a bone). The desired temperature is 180 to 185°F; since it will rise 5 to 10° while the turkey stands before carving, be careful not to cook bird past 185 degrees.

9. Lifting the turkey
Lifting the turkey out of the pan is always a challenge. Silicone gloves or potholders allow you to work hands on and are a worthwhile investment since you will need to tilt the bird enough to drain the juices from the body cavity into the pan before placing the turkey on

a platter. In addition, many brand names birds come with a lifting string harness that you can arrange on the bird prior to cooking. These work well if adjusted properly.

10. **Letting turkey rest**
When you remove the turkey from the oven, transfer it immediately to a warm serving platter and allow the turkey to sit for 30 to 40 minutes before carving; it will not cool off in this short time, and you'll get a juicier bird. While the turkey rests, make your giblet gravy.

Make Thanksgiving a truly memorable meal - *Last year at Christmas time, my mom went to my sister's house for the traditional holiday feast. Knowing how gullible my sister is, my mom decided to play a trick. She told my sister that she needed something from the store and asked if my sister wouldn't mind going out to get it.*

When my sister left the house, mom took the turkey out of the oven, removed the mixed stuffing, stuffed a Cornish hen, and inserted it into the turkey... then re-stuffed the turkey. She then placed the bird(s) back into the oven. When it was time for dinner, my sister pulled the turkey out of the oven and proceeded to remove the stuffing. When her serving spoon hit something, she reached in and pulled out the smaller bird.

With a look of total shock on her face, my mother exclaimed, "Barbara, you've cooked a pregnant bird!" At the reality of this horrifying news, my sister started to cry hysterically. It took the entire family almost two hours to convince her that turkeys lay eggs!

--Anonymous joke circling internet!

Quick and Easy Roast Turkey

-----Distinctly American Favorites-----

Depending on size, thaw turkey 2-5 days in the refrigerator, according to directions on package. Turkey must be fully defrosted without any ice inside or out in order to cook properly.

See "Talking Turkey" to determine how large a turkey to purchase for your meal

1	**name brand frozen turkey**
½	**teaspoon Kosher salt**
1	**teaspoon ground white pepper**
1½	**teaspoons garlic powder**
	spray cooking oil
1	**stick unsalted butter**

Necessary Equipment

• Heavy, light-colored roasting pan about 17 x 11½ x 2-inches or 2½-inches OR a large dark enamel roasting pan, depending on size of turkey

• Flat rack and kitchen string

• Dial style instant read thermometer

• Silicone gloves or pot holders for handling turkey

The day before you roast the turkey, remove the neck, heart and gizzard from the neck cavity and body of turkey. Rinse and pat dry. Use gizzard and neck to make Turkey Giblet Stock.

Quick and Easy Roast Turkey
Rinse turkey inside and out and pat dry. Cut off the tail, put turkey on a large platter and return to refrigerator. Cover with a damp paper towel and plastic wrap or aluminum foil, until next day. DO NOT do this any sooner than one day prior to cooking.

For a moist and succulent turkey, try this version.

Roast Turkey Extraordinaire
Rinse turkey inside and out and pat <u>damp</u> dry. Cut off the tail. Sprinkle Kosher salt <u>lightly</u> on skin of turkey making sure you *<u>do not get any on the inside</u>*. Put turkey on a large platter or pan and return, uncovered, to the refrigerator no more than 2 to 4 hours.

Use the following for both versions

When ready to roast, put oven rack in lower third of oven and preheat oven to 450 degrees. Remove turkey from refrigerator and rinse well inside and out. Dry thoroughly. Mix salt, pepper and garlic powder in a small bowl and sprinkle mixture evenly in turkey cavities and all over skin.

Spray roasting pan and rack with cooking spray. Spray backside of turkey all over with cooking spray and sit turkey on rack in roasting pan making sure it sits level. Put ⅔-stick butter in body cavity, and remaining ⅓ butter in the neck cavity. Fold neck skin under the body, then tuck the wing tips under the breast and tie the drumsticks together loosely, with kitchen string. Spray top and sides with oil.

Insert meat thermometer into fleshy part of thigh, close to but not touching the bone. Put turkey in oven with longer side of pan, and leg that has the thermometer in it, towards the back of oven. Roast uncovered, turning pan halfway through the cooking time so the other side of turkey, without thermometer, is in back of oven. If breast begins to brown too much, prepare an aluminum foil tent sprayed on the dull side with cooking spray and lay tent dull side down. Do not cover thermometer.

Roast approximately 8 minutes per pound, until thermometer registers 170 degrees. If you have used a foil tent, remove it the last 10 minutes. When turkey reaches correct internal temperature, remove from oven. Make a small slit on the inner side of the thigh without the thermometer and look at bone, there should be no pink, indicating that the turkey is fully cooked. With silicone gloves or potholders, carefully tilt the turkey and let the juices from the body cavity run into pan and set turkey on a serving platter.

Let the turkey stand for 30 minutes, the temperature of the thigh meat will rise to 180 degrees while standing. While turkey is standing, use pan juices to make gravy.

Roast Turkey Breast

-----Distinctly American Favorites-----

There are no giblets with breast so we recommend purchasing turkey necks from the grocer and make stock a day or two before using Turkey Giblet Stock recipe.

SERVES 4-6

6-8	**pound frozen turkey breast (with skin and bone)**
¼	**teaspoon salt**
½	**teaspoon ground white pepper**
1	**teaspoons garlic powder**
	spray cooking oil
½	**medium yellow or white onion**
	dab of butter

Necessary Equipment

• Heavy, light-colored roasting pan, glass baking dish, or enamel roasting pan

• V-rack

• Dial style instant read thermometer

• Silicone gloves or pot holders for handling turkey

The day you roast the breast, remove packaging from defrosted breast; rinse and pat damp dry with a towel.

Mix salt, pepper and garlic powder in a small bowl and sprinkle mixture all over turkey breast, on top and underneath. Spray the entire breast with cooking oil. If you prefer, you can rub cooking oil over entire breast and then season.

Put oven rack in lower third of oven and preheat oven to 450 degrees. Spray or grease the roasting pan and rack with more cooking oil.

If there is neck skin on breast, put the onion, lightly seasoned, and a dab of butter in neck cavity and fold neck skin under the body. You can also put a piece of lightly seasoned onion on rack underneath breast to help level it.

Insert meat thermometer into thickest part of breast, close to but not touching the bone. Place the pan with prepared breast, uncovered, in oven lengthwise with thermometer to the rear. Roast, turning pan halfway through the cooking time, so the thermometer is visible in front for the last half of roasting time. If breast begins to brown too much, prepare an aluminum foil tent sprayed on the dull side with cooking spray. Lay tent on top of breast, dull side down being careful not to cover thermometer.

Roast 1¼-1½ hours or until thermometer registers 170 degrees. If you used a foil tent, remove it the last 10 minutes. When turkey reaches correct internal temperature, remove from oven and move turkey to a serving platter.

Let the turkey stand for 30 minutes. The temperature of the breast will rise to about 180 degrees while standing. While turkey is standing, use pan juices to make gravy.

A family picnic - *can consist of what each individual wants to eat. Hit the grocery store with a list or the children helping find stuff. Don't worry about the nutrition labels for this one; just go for the gusto and the taste. The oldest wants a hot dog and the youngest wants macaroni and cheese? Fix'em up. Potato chips, soft drinks, Viennese sausage and crackers, whatever...the idea is to have fun with the food and make it a memorable time. Take everybody for ice cream afterwards or take them home to top it off with a make-your-own-Sundae for dessert. Take lots of pictures so they can commemorate the event.*
  Do it every once in a while to keep the spirits up and develop those family bonds.

Roast Turkey Giblet Gravy

-----Distinctly American Favorites-----

<u>Do not</u> throw away the pan drippings! Giblets may have been used in your dressing, which I recommend baking separately in an oven proof casserole dish. Even without actual giblets, gravy will have their flavor and will be excellent.

Makes 2-4 cups

> **pan juices from roasted turkey**
>
> **giblet stock with giblets, made the day before**
>
> **salt and pepper to taste**

Natural Gravy

Pour turkey pan juices into a 2-quart glass measuring container or heat proof bowl. Do not wash pan. When juices have settled and fat has risen to top, 1-2 minutes, remove most but not all of the fat and discard.

If giblet stock was previously refrigerated, remove now and discard congealed fat from top. Put stock in a 3-quart saucepan and heat to boiling. Pour hot stock into turkey pan and deglaze pan by scraping up brown bits. Pour stock from deglazed turkey pan back into saucepan; add pan juices from glass container, and any juices on the platter with turkey. Bring to a moderate boil over medium-high heat. Salt and pepper to taste. Serve hot.

¼	**cornstarch**
½	**cup water**
	salt and pepper

Natural Gravy Thickened with Cornstarch

In a small container, stir together cornstarch and water until there are no lumps. Add to hot liquid in saucepan, stirring constantly to avoid formation of lumps. Turn heat to low and simmer uncovered, stirring several times, for about 10-15 minutes. Adjust seasonings to taste.

4-6	**tablespoons fat**
¼	**cup all-purpose flour**
	salt and pepper

Brown Gravy with a Roux

Spray a heavy 3-quart saucepan with oil, remove fat that has risen on turkey juices in glass container and put 4-6 tablespoons fat into skillet over medium heat. Discard remaining fat. Whisk flour into fat in saucepan. Cook flour and fat mixture over medium high heat, stirring constantly until golden brown, 3-5 minutes, making a roux.

Add hot stock in turkey pan to roux, whisking or stirring constantly to prevent lumps, then add turkey pan juices and giblets from glass container, plus any juices that have accumulated on platter with turkey. Simmer uncovered over low heat, about 15 minutes, stirring several times.

Adjust seasonings according to taste.

Turkey Giblet Stock

-----Distinctly American Favorites-----

Even if you don't like giblets themselves - you will love this gravy base. One way to keep your gravy from dripping out of your gravy boat or cream pitcher is to dab a little butter on the spout. This will save your tablecloth.

Makes 7 cups stock

	giblets from turkey
2	**tablespoons vegetable oil**
	kosher salt
	ground black pepper
1	**large white or yellow onion, quartered**
1	**tablespoon minced garlic**
4	**cups hot water**
1	**(14-ounce) can chicken broth**

Read entire recipe in full before beginning preparation.

Use the giblets that you like, which can be one or all, depending on your preference. Using all of the giblets will add more flavor to your stock. Ordinarily, you will find the neck packet in the body cavity and the other giblets under the neck skin at the full end of the breast.

Spray a 3-4 quart heavy saucepan with oil, add 2 tablespoons vegetable oil and heat over high heat until hot but not smoking. Lightly dust giblets, neck and gizzard, with salt and pepper. Turn heat to medium high and brown neck and other giblets for about 10 minutes. Add the onion and continue to brown all for about 5 more minutes, stirring constantly. Add garlic the last minute or two of the browning process and stir constantly being careful not to overcook garlic. When giblets and seasoning are browned, add water and broth, ½ teaspoon salt, and 1 teaspoon pepper. Bring to a boil, cover and reduce heat to low. Simmer until very tender, about 2½ hours. Cool stock uncovered on stove for one but not more than 1½ hours or you chance your stock going sour.

Pour stock through a large sieve into a large

oven proof bowl in order to remove solids. Set bowl in refrigerator, uncovered, while you prepare giblets. Dice gizzard and throw away hard connective tissue. Remove meat from neck, discard bones and dice meat as necessary. Discard onions and garlic from sieve. Return prepared giblets to the stock, cover, and chill overnight (if possible). In the morning, skim off fat that has congealed on the top.

NOTE: You can use giblets and/or 1-2 cups of stock in turkey dressing. If you do use some of the stock for your dressing, add an equivalent amount of water or chicken broth to remaining stock.

Let's get "cultural" - *Have one meal a month be a cultural experience and designate one member of the family to be the host for the meal. They can pick the culture, research it and plan the gathering. Maybe they will want to do a meal of India eating the flavors or style of India and telling a little about the food customs of that culture, or possible a Mexican Cinco de Mayo, or a Hawaiian Luau.*

The internet is a great place for the hostess to get information and plan, its simple enough for children to do.

Bread Crumbs

-----*Distinctly American Favorites*-----

Home made bread crumbs have a freshness that is far superior to store-bought. You can experiment with other kinds of bread such as wheat, sour dough or rye remembering that each bread has its own distinct flavor.

Italian or other substantial bread

For use as thickener:

Homemade bread crumbs can be used to thicken sauces also, in place of flour or cornstarch.

Add the crumbs sparingly and cook sauce for a few extra minutes, adding more crumbs as necessary. Strain sauce before using, being sure to press or squeeze liquid out of crumbs.

Allow bread to dry in an open, dry place – moisture will cause mold to grow so avoid damp areas. If you have a gas oven with a pilot light you can leave bread in oven overnight in the oven.

When dried, either grate bread on a box grater or break into chunks and pulse in a blender or process in a food processor. Sift and reprocess large remaining pieces or crush them between wax paper with a rolling pen.

Store crumbs in an airtight container.

For seasoned bread crumbs, combine with seasonings such as grated Parmesan cheese, garlic powder, dried basil and/or parsley, salt and pepper of choice, thyme. Let your imagination or your recipe be your guide.

Peggy's Basic Flour Seasoning

-----Distinctly American Favorites-----

This is easy to make and have prepared in the freezer or in an airtight canister.

Makes seasoning for 6-12 cups of flour

1½	tablespoons garlic powder
1	tablespoon paprika
1	tablespoon salt
1	tablespoon onion powder
1	tablespoon ground white pepper
½	teaspoon turmeric
1	teaspoon dried cilantro or parsley, powdered
½	teaspoon ground cayenne, optional
1	teaspoon Cajun seasoning, optional

Mix all ingredients and store in an airtight container.

Use one tablespoon seasoning to a cup of flour, or according to taste.

For a more spicy flavor coating – add either ½ teaspoon ground cayenne or 1 teaspoon Cajun seasoning.

It's a grill thing: *Grill small steaks, wings, sausage on a stick, hot dogs or hamburgers, or whatever the budget and taste preference allows and eat outside on paper plates and napkins with plastic utensils. Get a special tablecloth and maybe a special apron, provide cold drinks and favorite chips and dips possibly surprising the group with homemade cookies, ice cream sundaes or watermelon for dessert. The goal is to have fun and share a family meal in a different atmosphere not reserved only for company.*

Spiced Nuts

-----Distinctly American Favorites-----

This provides a marvelous crusty coasting on various meat dishes such as shrimp, chicken or fish.

Makes two cups

2	**cups pecans or peanuts**
2	**tablespoons hot pepper sauce**
2	**tablespoons Worcestershire sauce**

Preheat oven to 250 degrees.

Put all ingredients in a medium bowl and toss well.

Spread on a baking sheet and roast, stirring every 15 minutes, until dry and crispy, about 30 to 45 minutes. Watch carefully so they do not burn or dry out too much.

Cool to room temperature and store in a covered container.

We have all been guilty of taking someone for granted. When we stop and think about it, we know we love them and appreciate all they do, but we also expect them to know that without us telling them. Every once in a while a person likes to be appreciated, just because…whether it is the cook of the family, the breadwinner or someone else. Many of us will go out to eat to celebrate a special occasion. But how about doing something for non-special times? An interesting idea is to purchase some meaningful greeting cards and hide them around the house in various surprise locations. Put them under plates at meal times, or in a bowl or container that might be used as a serving dish when the meal is served. If you are not the cook, put one in among the spices so it will fall out when a spice is selected. Other places that can be used are drawers in the kitchen, the freezing compartment of the refrigerator, in a clothes dryer, in a book that is being read by the person, inside a shoe or other article of clothing and the list goes on and on. Don't rely on the card itself to carry the message of love and caring, always jot a few words of affection and fondness and explain that the occasion is "just because…"

Flowers are a nice gesture and should be used as well, but the card game is a little different and less expensive alternative and may even express your feelings more nicely

Warm and Tender
Soup, Salad & Veggies

Love is a many flavored thing...

Contents

-----Warm and Tender ~ Soup, Salad & Veggies-----

Lite Bean Soup

-----*Warm and Tender ~ Soup, Salad & Veggies*-----

Feeling down? Is there a chill in the air or in your body? Try this great warmer upper. It's even better the next day after flavors have blended. Skim fat off top before serving for a lighter version.

SERVES 6-8

1	**pound dried white or navy beans**
1½	**pounds pork (country ribs or shoulder)**
	salt, pepper and garlic powder
3	**tablespoons extra virgin olive oil or other cooking oil**
1	**medium to large white onion, chopped chunky**
4	**cloves garlic**
8	**cups boiling water**
1	**teaspoon ground pepper of choice**
1	**teaspoon salt**
1	**bay leaf**
7	**ounces baby spinach**

Sort and rinse beans under cold water and pick out rocks. Place in 4-quart pot and cover with water several inches above beans. Bring to a boil, reduce heat and simmer for 5 minutes. Turn off heat and soak beans 1 to 4 hours, adding additional water if necessary.

Move oven shelf to second-highest level and preheat to 450 degrees. Spray a roasting pan. Coat a roaster rack with oil and place inside the roaster. Coat both sides of pork with oil and dust with salt, pepper and garlic powder. Place pork in a single layer on the prepared rack. Roast until pork begins to brown, turning pork once. (This will remove excess fat from the pork and provide a hearty flavor to the soup.) Remove pan from oven, defat and chop when cool.

Thoroughly drain beans and set aside.

In a 4-quart or larger pot, heat olive oil over medium high heat, until hot but not smoking. Add onion and sauté until the onion begins to soften. Smash garlic cloves with the flat side of a large knife, and remove peel. Add garlic and pork to stockpot and sauté about 2 minutes, being careful not to brown the garlic.

Add 8 cups boiling water, pepper, salt, bay leaf, and beans. Bring to a full boil over high heat and then reduce the heat. Simmer until beans are slightly tender but still crunchy, adding water as necessary to keep water level at least 2 to 3 inches above beans. Stir every 10-15 minutes. When beans are cooked, remove bay leaf. Season with salt and pepper to taste.

Bring liquid back to a boil. Stir in spinach. Return to full boil and reduce heat to medium-low. Boil gently for approximately 30 minutes, stirring every 10 minutes. Adjust seasonings as necessary.

Romantic picnic idea can be a great "togetherness" for just the two of you – *even we senior citizens get the hang of it. If the weather is right, prepare your favorite outdoor food like fried chicken, cole slaw, potato salad, marinated mushrooms and have a little cooler with champagne, wine or other drinks. If you have silver goblets chill them in the cooler. When we were courting, my husband and I often went to a secluded beach in Galveston where we listened to music, fed each other our picnic tidbits and sipped champagne. He proposed to me on the beach one evening with a cold wind blowing off the water and me giggling trying to hold down a blanket with one hand and keeping another blanket over me with the other. He kept trying to hand me a glass of champagne, but I was too busy to take it. Finally in exasperation he helped me settle the blankets down and quoted this little ditty "I'm not worried about the future, I don't care about the past; I don't need to be your first love, just want to be your last." Then he asked me to marry him. Of course I was touched, and finally said yes after thinking it over for a few seconds. Then he toasted me and asked if I were going to drink my champagne. So, I dutifully sipped at it, even though I was getting pretty chilly. He finally had to tell me to look in the bottom of the silver goblet and when I did I found a beautiful engagement ring nestled and waiting for me. That made it real, and we got married a few months later.*

Roasted Rib Soup

This warm and wonderful soup is sure to revive the spirit and satisfy. It serves many, depending on size of servings, and holds for several days in the refrigerator. Delicious with hot crusty bread.

SERVES 6-8

1	**onion, sliced thick (three slices for medium onion, four for large onion) - Do not separate rings**
	garlic powder
	coarse ground black pepper
6	**large beef ribs (fresh cut when possible, preferably Angus beef)**
	salt
2	**(14-ounce) cans chicken broth**
2	**cups water**
½	**(14.5-ounce) can petite diced tomatoes with liquid**
1	**tablespoon fresh minced garlic**
1	**tablespoon finely minced fresh parsley, or equivalent dried**
1	**cup carrots, chunky chopped**
1	**large green bell pepper, chunky chopped**
1	**cup (or more) shredded cabbage for slaw, or 1 small cabbage**
1	**can or 1-2 cups frozen green baby lima beans**

Preheat oven to 450 degrees. Spray a baking pan (approximately 9 x 13-inches) with cooking oil. Spray one side of onion slices with oil, turn over and season with garlic powder and ground pepper, then spray with oil.

Lay onion slices in a line on bottom of baking pan.

Season ribs on each side with garlic powder, black pepper, and a light dusting of salt, then spray with oil. Lay ribs in pan over onion slices with curve of rib up. Place pan of ribs in oven and roast approximately 45 minutes – until lightly brown on outside.

While ribs are roasting, prepare other ingredients. Put chicken broth in a 5 to 6-quart pot on stove. Add water and tomatoes, garlic and parsley and bring to boil, turn heat to low and keep hot until ribs are cooked.

When ribs are browned, add ribs and onion slices (not drippings in pan) to the stock pot, season with salt and pepper to taste, and bring to boil. Reduce heat to simmer, cover and cook until ribs are tender, about 45 minutes to 1 hour depending on quality of meat.

Add carrots and cook an additional ten minutes. Remove ribs from stock and cool to room temperature.

When using whole cabbage, cut cabbage in chunks or slice as for slaw. If using canned beans, drain and rinse lima beans.

While ribs are cooling, add green pepper, cabbage and lima beans to stock pot. Bring to boil, reduce heat and simmer 20 minutes. While this cooks, remove meat from fat and bones and add meat to soup. Adjust seasonings again, as necessary.

If you prefer other vegetables, use your favorites to substitute for those listed. Rather than delete those like onions, bell pepper, and/or carrots, process them so they will dissolve, otherwise you will not have the flavor you desire – they give the soup that great taste along with the rib flavor.

This hearty beef soup may be made the day before or just prior to serving. If made in advance, chill soup and skim rendered beef fat that congeals on top.

Picnics are a treat for many families. *Drive to a local park, or a recreational area near home on a weekend or a summer evening when there is more light. If there isn't time or a favorite spot, have the picnic in the backyard. No backyard? Spread a blanket in the living room and let the family have their picnic at home.*

Veggie Soup Your Way

-----Warm and Tender ~ Soup, Salad & Veggies-----

Not only is this soup good, it is good for you - the chicken and vegetables make this a healthy meal hard to beat. However, if you want a vegan soup, simply leave the meat out and use vegetable broth in place of chicken.

SERVES 6-8

½	rotisserie chicken, boned and skinned, or 2 chicken breasts*, optional
1	tablespoon olive oil
	salt, pepper and garlic powder
1	(10-ounce) can tomatoes, Rotel, other diced tomatoes, or V-8 Juice
	if not using Rotel, add ½ teaspoon coarse ground pepper or red pepper flakes
2	(14.5 ounce) cans chicken broth
1	large onion, sliced thin
4	cloves garlic smashed
1	teaspoon celery seed, or 2 stalks celery, washed and cut in chunks
1	tablespoon minced parsley
1	cup frozen green peas
2	red potatoes, washed and cut in chunks
½	cup shredded carrots
2	cups shredded cabbage
1	cup raw small pasta of choice

If using raw chicken, raise oven rack to highest level and turn oven to broil. Coat chicken with oil and dust with salt, pepper and garlic powder. Place chicken in an oven proof baking dish sprayed with cooking oil and broil 5 minutes on each side (or until golden brown on outside). Remove from oven.

Now for the easy part. The vegetables listed are some of my soup favorites which I have at home. You should decide what you like (maybe corn, zucchini, green peppers) and have available and go from there.

Put chicken broth, onion, garlic, celery, parsley and peas into a soup pot or Dutch oven. Bring to boil over high heat, then turn down to low, cover and simmer until onion is tender.

*I like rotisserie chicken for soup because it is already cooked and has more flavor. Buy the cooked chicken, de-bone and skin it and freeze until ready to use. You can tie the bones and skin in cheesecloth and add to the soup until all is cooked. This imparts a lot of flavor to the liquid and the bag is easy to remove.

Put chicken into the liquid mixture. If using the raw chicken, cook about 30 minutes with lid on.

Add the potatoes and carrots, and more water if necessary, bring back to a boil, lower heat, cover and cook about 10 more minutes. Stir in the cabbage and pasta and continue cooking until everything is tender.

It is best not to use more than six cups of vegetables.

Soup may be served hot or at room temperature.

Hobo parties are fun, informal and easy to arrange. *Each guest dresses informally with their vision of what a hobo looks like, and each brings a can of vegetables. The host can have a big, slow cooking soup pot with some meat in it for starters. As each guest arrives, they open their cans and pour them into the pot. Served with hot bread and some salt and pepper, the flavorful slumgullion is often the hit of the party.*

Fruit Salad and Dressing

A great pick-me-up with an iced drink on a hot summer day. A couple of mini-muffins with whipped cream cheese make it an elegant treat.

SERVES 4-6

4-6   cups of apple and grapes

You can also include any combination of the following:

>   **canned mandarin orange segments, drained well**
>
>   **raspberries**
>
>   **kiwi**
>
>   **banana**

6   slices fresh bacon, fried crisp, drained, and crumbled

1   cup real mayonnaise (not salad dressing or fat free)

¾   cup fine granulated sugar

4   tablespoons red wine vinegar

½   cup walnuts or pecans

2   teaspoons poppy seeds, optional

Rinse and/or peel and cut fruit, as necessary, in bite sized pieces in a large bowl.

Make salad dressing by mixing together, in a separate bowl, bacon, mayonnaise, sugar, vinegar, nuts and poppy seeds (if preferred). Pour a generous amount over fruit and toss.

Store salad in refrigerator until chilled, for a minimum of 30 minutes.

Serve as is or over salad greens.

Fruity Tooty Salad

This is one of my favorites and is good with any entree. Delicious as a side salad or entrée with chicken or shrimp.

SERVES 3-4

10   ounces or more crisp chilled lettuce of choice, broken in bite size pieces

1   (8-ounce) can mandarin orange slices, chilled and drained well

1   cup dried cherries or craisans

1   cup walnut or lightly toasted almond pieces

1   large crisp apple, cut in bite size pieces

   crumbled cheese, bleu or feta, optional

2   slices fresh crisp fried bacon, crumbled

1   cup miniature marshmallows

1-2   cups boiled and peeled or breaded shrimp, or cooked cubed chicken breast

   bottled salad dressing of choice (such as Raspberry Hazelnut)

Put all ingredients in a large salad bowl and toss well. Serve with dressing of choice.

Honeybunch Chicken Salad

Sure to be a crowd pleaser particularly when served with hot Tuscan bread. If you prefer chunky chicken salad, all ingredients may be cut accordingly.

SERVES 1-2

1	**(10-ounce) can Premium Chunk White Chicken in water**
1	**large sweet and crisp apple, cored, peeled and chopped to your size of choice**
¼	**cup finely minced celery, or 1 teaspoon celery seed**
¼	**cup mayonnaise**
1	**tablespoon extra fine granulated white sugar or honey**
½	**teaspoon salt**
¼	**teaspoon ground pepper, white or black**
¼	**cup finely chopped nuts of choice, optional**
¼	**cup finely chopped water chestnuts (for crunch), optional**

Thoroughly drain chicken and dice in electric chopper or break apart with fork.

Mix all ingredients and stir well. Adjust seasonings. Chill until ready to use.

Shrimp and Spinach Salad

-----*Warm and Tender ~ Soup, Salad & Veggies*-----

Light but zingy, perfect for lunches. Great served with warm soup or pasta side dish.

SERVES 2-4

½	**medium sweet or white onion, sliced thin**
2	**tablespoons hot sauce, Tabasco preferred**
1	**cup sweet grape or cherry tomatoes, oven roasted**
1	**cup flour seasoned to taste with salt, pepper, and ½ teaspoon garlic powder**
¼	**cup spiced nuts or roasted pistachio nuts**
½	**pound peeled and de-veined boiled shrimp, chilled**
1	**pound baby spinach, cleaned and stems removed**
¼	**cup salad dressing of choice**

Marinate onions in hot sauce for 30 minutes.

While onions marinate, roast tomatoes in 450 degree oven for about 5 minutes, set aside to cool.

Preheat deep fryer to 350 degrees. If you don't have a deep fryer, use a skillet with hot oil. Toss onions in seasoned flour and fry until lightly golden. Remove and drain on paper towel.

In a large mixing bowl, toss nuts, shrimp, spinach and fried onion. Drizzle salad dressing over all and toss again.

Serve alone or as an accompaniment.

Simple Italian Salad

Buon Appetito!

SERVES 4-6

8	cups salad greens - romaine, iceberg, baby spinach or a combination of all
½	cup olive oil
4	Roma tomatoes, sliced ¼-inch thick
4	ounces finely shredded Mozzarella cheese, or fresh Mozzarella balls cut in half
3	tablespoons or more balsamic or salad vinegar, to taste, optional
	Kosher salt and coarse ground black pepper
	croutons, optional
	rinsed and pitted black, kalamata or green olives, optional

Gently toss greens with olive oil.

Add tomatoes, cheese, and optional vinegar and toss again. Season with salt and pepper to taste.

Add croutons and/or olives if preferred.

Sweet Pea Salad

A great side dish that can be prepared and kept in the refrigerator for several days until shared. Try serving with Honeybunch Chicken Salad and crackers.

SERVES 4-6

6	hardboiled eggs, peeled and chopped small
1	small roasted red pepper, cleaned, peeled and diced
2	(15-ounce) cans sweet green peas, drained (or 3 cups frozen peas cooked and drained)
2	tablespoons white or red onion, minced
2	stalks celery, finely chopped
¼	cup mayonnaise, Hellman's original or canola
	salt and pepper to taste

Combine all ingredients in a large bowl and chill thoroughly.

Have an "I like (or love) you because " meal - *Use the best china and linens. Fix the honoree's favorite foods and make small notes that begin "I Like You Because..." with one or two ideas on it. Put the note on the person's plate, or in the water glass, or in the napkin, and be sure to fix their favorite dessert (hopefully shaped like a heart). Maybe you can get the whole family to participate and write a note for the occasion. Not only does the food provide comfort and nurturing but the note is a tangible affirmation the person is apt to keep for years to come. This can be done for no particular reason or when someone needs a pick me up.*

Wilted Spinach with Shrimp Salad

-----Warm and Tender ~ Soup, Salad & Veggies-----

Feeling wilted yourself? Use this recipe to perk up and get going again.

SERVES 2-4

½	medium sweet or white onion, sliced thin
4	large mushrooms (4 ounces), cleaned and sliced thin
2	tablespoons olive oil
1	clove garlic
½-¾	pound large, raw shrimp
2	tablespoons cornstarch
¼	teaspoon each salt, pepper and garlic powder
1	pound baby spinach, cleaned and stems removed
1	hardboiled egg, optional
4	slices bacon
	Kosher salt and coarse ground pepper
1	tablespoon red wine vinegar

Set aside in separate containers. In small bowl, set aside olive oil. Peel and smash the garlic and put in the oil. Set aside.

Peel, de-vein and butterfly the shrimp. Lightly dust shrimp with mixture of cornstarch, salt, pepper and garlic powder. Set aside.

If necessary, wash spinach and remove stems. Put in a large salad bowl and set aside. Mince or grate boiled egg and set aside (optional).

Cut bacon in ½-inch pieces and fry in a large 10 to 12-inch skillet. When crisp, take bacon out and drain on paper towel. Pour off all grease drippings except 3-4 tablespoons. Remove garlic from oil, mince garlic and set aside. Add garlic oil to bacon grease and heat over medium heat to hot but not smoking. Add mushrooms and shrimp to oil and sauté about two minutes, stirring frequently until shrimp is pink and opaque white. Add garlic and remove skillet from heat.

Drizzle hot oil and skillet ingredients over spinach and toss; season with Kosher salt and coarse ground pepper and toss again. Drizzle vinegar over all. Add onions, bacon pieces and toss. Adjust seasonings if necessary. Sprinkle egg over all. Serve immediately.

Sizzling Brussels Sprouts

-----Warm and Tender ~ Soup, Salad & Veggies-----

Try this instead of just steaming with butter! Brussels sprouts are not my favorite food, but cooked like this I love them! For variety, allow sprouts to cook a little longer until the outer leaves are brown and slightly crunchy. Serve hot.

SERVES 4-6

1½	**pounds fresh, firm brussels sprouts, cut in quarters or halved**
2	**tablespoons olive oil, extra-virgin has more flavor**
2	**cloves fresh garlic, smashed and peeled**
2	**tablespoons unsalted butter**
¼	**teaspoon red pepper flakes or coarse ground black pepper**
¼	**teaspoon salt**

Butter sauce

1	**teaspoon lemon juice, optional**
2	**tablespoons melted butter**
½	**teaspoon minced parsley, or ¼ teaspoon dried parsley flakes**
¼	**teaspoon salt**

Rinse and drain sprouts and remove any dark outer leaves. Cut the sprouts in quarters or halves depending upon the size of the sprout in order to have similar size pieces. With the tip of your knife, remove the cone shaped core from each piece, discard core, and drop prepared sprouts in a bowl.

Put the oil and garlic in a 10-inch or larger skillet or sauté pan, over medium heat. Cook and brown the garlic for about 4 minutes, stirring often. Remove garlic from oil and discard (or use in another recipe), add butter and sprouts. Spread sprouts in pan and season with pepper and salt.

Cover the skillet and cook sprouts. The oil should be hot enough for sprouts to sizzle but not brown. To prevent browning, lower heat. About every 2 minutes, remove cover and turn sprouts over with a large spoon, cover again and continue cooking until sprouts are soft, or approximately 10 minutes total. While sprouts cook, prepare butter sauce by combing all ingredients in bottom of warm serving dish.

Transfer cooked sprouts to the prepared serving dish. Serve hot.

Caramelized Cauliflower

Get out of the rut of plain steamed cauliflower and enjoy this treat. For more flavor, sprinkle seasoned bread crumbs or shredded cheese over top of cooked cauliflower before serving.

SERVES 4

1	**1½-2 pound cauliflower**
3	**tablespoons olive oil**
4	**tablespoons unsalted butter**
½	**teaspoon salt**
¼	**teaspoon ground white pepper**
¼	**cup seasoned bread crumbs, optional**
¼	**cup of your favorite shredded cheese**

Remove all outer leaves from the base of the cauliflower. Separate big florets, either snapping them off or cutting them from the core stem. Cut the florets in 1-inch thick chunks as equally as possible. Discard all stems.

Put oil and one tablespoon of butter in a 10-inch or larger skillet, with a lid, and put on stove over medium heat. Add the cauliflower to skillet, then sprinkle cauliflower with salt and pepper, and cover. Turn heat to medium low.

After about 4 minutes, remove cover, turn the florets over with a large spoon, and cover again. If pieces have not begun to brown, turn heat up slightly. Let the cauliflower cook and caramelize slowly, turning the pieces every few minutes and cooking for 12-15 minutes in all.

Add 3 tablespoons butter to pan and toss cauliflower gently until butter has melted and coated all pieces. Add more salt if desired. Pour cauliflower onto a warm serving dish. Top with bread crumbs or shredded cheese and serve hot.

Corn Casserole

An old fashioned favorite that is sure to win your heart! If you do not have fiesta corn, use an equal amount of regular canned whole kernel corn or defrosted frozen whole kernel corn, and ¼- ½ cup minced green bell pepper.

SERVES 4-6

1	**(15-ounce) can Fiesta corn, drained well**
1	**(15-ounce) can creamed corn**
1	**cup Club crackers, crushed**
½	**cup whole milk**
½-¾	**cup minced onion**
½	**teaspoon salt**
1	**teaspoon ground black pepper**
3	**tablespoons unsalted butter, melted**
2	**large eggs, beaten**

Preheat oven to 375 degrees. Grease or butter a 2-quart oven proof casserole dish.

Mix all ingredients, except eggs, in a large bowl. Stir thoroughly, then add beaten eggs and blend. Pour all ingredients into a casserole dish and bake 40-45 minutes, until a knife inserted in the center comes out clean.

Serve warm.

Rotate meal planning and preparation responsibilities with older children. *Give older children some time in the kitchen to learn how to prepare a portion or even all of a meal. I know one family who had several teenagers and to help them learn basic survival skills, they took weekly turns at planning an evening dinner menu and preparing it for the family. Of course you have to outlaw the shortcuts of individual frozen dinners or "fish sticks and tater tots" as the primary entree of the day. A good way to encourage cooking is to have a house rule that if you cook you don't have to do the dishes.*

Corn Ragout

-----Warm and Tender ~ Soup, Salad & Veggies-----

Corn lovers arise - your tastebuds will love you for this! Yum! In a pinch, substitute frozen whole kernel corn and cook slightly longer, however, nothing tastes quite like fresh corn.

SERVES 2-4

3	**tablespoons butter**
4	**cups freshly shucked sweet corn, about 8 ears**
3	**medium jalapeno peppers, seeded, minced**
1	**tablespoon onion, finely minced**
	salt and pepper to taste
1	**tablespoon fresh cilantro, chopped (or 1 teaspoon dried)**
2-3	**tablespoons fresh plum tomato, diced**
	fresh cilantro
2	**strips bacon, crisp, crumbled, optional**

Spray sauté pan with oil and heat over medium heat. Add one tablespoon butter. Be careful not to burn the butter. Place corn, jalapeno and onion in pan. Stir constantly, season with salt and pepper. When corn is completely hot (1½ to 2 minutes) stir in the remaining butter and add chopped cilantro. Cook until all butter has melted. Season to taste. Garnish with lightly salted tomato, optional bacon, and fresh cilantro.

Corn ragout can be served as an individual side or spooned over crab cakes, chops, or chicken. Let your imagination be your guide and enjoy!

Corncakes

Be still my heart! This is simply divine! Be sure not to turn your cakes over too soon. It could cause them to lose the round shape and not cook evenly.

SERVES 2-4

3	slices crisp cooked bacon, crumbled, or fresh bacon bits
4	tablespoons butter
6	large eggs
1	(15-ounce) can creamed corn
1	tablespoon each green pepper and jalapeno pepper, finely minced substitute ½ teaspoon ground black or white pepper for jalapeno pepper
14	saltine-type crackers, crunched up to small pieces and crumbs
¼	cup shredded cheese, optional
1	tablespoon cooking oil

Fry bacon until crisp and set aside. Crumble when cool. Melt the butter and set aside to cool.

In a medium bowl, whisk eggs until well blended. Stir in ½ of the butter (2 tablespoons), crumbled bacon, and remaining ingredients except butter and oil.

Heat a clean non-stick skillet to medium high, add remaining 2 tablespoons of butter and cooking oil, and pour batter as you would pancakes. Cook until dry around edges, being careful not to turn corn cake over until cooked thoroughly on the first side. Flip the corn cake and finish cooking to golden brown. Continue to make corn cakes until all batter is used.

Eat with butter, salt and pepper, or warm syrup, honey or ketchup.

Shrimply Corn

Oh my - this is truly food of the Gods for shrimp and corn lovers. My husband thinks corn is a separate food group and this recipe just verifies his opinion!

SERVES 4

1	**pound large fresh or defrosted frozen shrimp, shelled and de-veined***
	salt
	coarse ground black pepper
	garlic powder
2	**tablespoons butter**
2	**tablespoons olive oil**
2	**ears fresh corn, kernels cut off the cobb**
1	**slice bacon, cut small**
2	**tablespoons finely minced shallots**
1	**teaspoon minced garlic**
½	**cup heavy whipping cream**
1	**teaspoon red pepper flakes**
1	**(10-ounce) can Rotel tomatoes**
1	**teaspoon finely minced fresh cilantro or parsley, or ½ teaspoon dried**

*Fresh scallops can be substituted for shrimp if available

Lightly dust shrimp (or scallops) with salt, pepper and garlic powder. Put butter and olive oil in a non-stick skillet and heat to hot. Add pieces of meat one at a time and sauté approximately 1½ minutes per side until beginning to brown. While shrimp (or scallops) cook, cut corn kernels from the cob, then remove meat from the pan to a bowl and set aside.

Heat skillet again and add the cut bacon, shallots and garlic. Stir and sauté about 1 minute or until bacon throws fat and begins to crisp.

Add corn kernels to skillet and stir in the whipping cream. Heat thoroughly while stirring up brown bits to deglaze the bottom of pan. Add shrimp (or scallops) and any juice that has accumulated. Stir again. Add red pepper flakes, Rotel tomatoes (do not drain), and cilantro and simmer for about 3 minutes.

Serve alone or over warm al dente pasta or rice of choice with a green salad.

Hearty Mashed Potatoes

Everybody's favorite - just like mom made. To slow down the process of your potatoes growing "eyes", keep your potatoes stored in a dark, cool, dry place with good ventilation.

SERVES 5-6

5-6	**medium russet potatoes (2½ pounds), peeled and rinsed, cut in ½-inch slices**
1	**teaspoon salt**
4	**tablespoons room temperature unsalted butter**
1	**tablespoon fresh parsley, finely minced or 1 teaspoon dried parsley**
1	**cup whole milk or 8 ounces light whipping cream, warmed**
	salt and pepper to taste

Put potatoes in a large pot and cover with water to about 1 inch above potatoes. Potatoes will lose their flavor if cooked in too much water. Thirty minutes prior to mealtime, add 1 teaspoon salt to water and boil potatoes just until tender, test with fork after about 15 minutes. (*IMPORTANT*: Be careful not to overcook potatoes. If they get too tender they will be like glue.) Drain and return potatoes to the hot pot. Dry over medium heat for no more than one minute to evaporate excess water.

Remove pot from heat and mash (do not whip) potatoes in the pot leaving some small lumps; then add butter, parsley, half the milk or cream and a dash pepper, stir gently. Add more milk, a few teaspoons at a time, until potatoes are the consistency you like. Taste again and add salt and pepper to taste.

Serve warm.

Parsley and Peppercorn Potatoes

-----Warm and Tender ~ Soup, Salad & Veggies-----

Why this is no longer an every week staple, I don't know. It is so easy and flavorful and is a favorite of all who try it.

SERVES 4-6

6	**large red potatoes**
1½	**teaspoon salt**
1	**stick unsalted butter**
½	**teaspoon cracked black peppercorn pepper**
½	**cup fresh parsley, finely chopped**
1	**teaspoon minced garlic**

Scrub potatoes and poke holes in various places on each potato with a fork. Put potatoes in a medium pot, cover with water, add one teaspoon salt and boil gently until tender, about 30 minutes after coming to a boil.

While potatoes are boiling, melt butter with pepper, parsley, garlic and ½ teaspoon salt in a small saucepan and simmer on lowest heat for 2 minutes. Turn heat off.

When potatoes are tender, remove from heat and drain. Transfer potatoes to a serving bowl, and using a fork, break each potato into several pieces. Drizzle seasoned butter over potatoes and toss. Add more salt and pepper to your taste. Serve warm.

Sweet Potato Delight

-----Warm and Tender ~ Soup, Salad & Veggies-----

The flavor will awaken the sweet potato lover in you! It is equally delicious chilled. May be prepared early in the day and assembled when ready to bake.

SERVES 4-6

1½	**cups baked sweet potatoes without skin, mashed**
2	**eggs**
1	**(14-ounce) can Eagle Brand condensed milk**
1	**cup oats**
1	**cup walnuts or pecans, chopped**
½	**cup all purpose flour**
1	**cup dark brown sugar**
½	**teaspoon cinnamon**
	dash salt
½	**pound butter (2 sticks)**

Preheat oven to 350 degrees. In a large bowl, stir together mashed sweet potatoes, eggs and condensed milk and set aside.

Heavily butter a 9 x 13-inch baking dish. Sprinkle ½ cup oats and ½ cup nuts in the bottom of pan.

In another bowl, mix remaining oats, flour, sugar, cinnamon, and salt. Cut sticks of butter into dry ingredients until mixture is crumbly.

Spoon potato mixture into greased pan; top with crumbled mixture, then with remaining nuts. Take a butter knife and cut into potatoes here and there to mix in a little of the topping (like streusel).

Bake at 350 degrees for about 45 minutes.

Cool slightly and serve warm with a dollop of whipped cream.

Sweet Potato Soufflé

-----Warm and Tender ~ Soup, Salad & Veggies-----

Hold on to your spoons - this is decadent! Does not require refrigeration. To use as a dessert, put one scoop into a small dessert dish or saucer and top with Dessert Praline Topping and/or Whipped Cream.

SERVES 4

2	**pounds (2 large) sweet potatoes**
2	**tablespoons water**
1½	**cups granulated white sugar**
½	**cup light brown sugar**
2	**teaspoons baking powder**
⅛	**teaspoon salt**
⅛	**teaspoon ground cinnamon**
3½	**level tablespoons all-purpose flour**
1½	**teaspoon vanilla extract**
4	**large eggs**
½	**cup softened butter**
1	**tablespoon white confectioner's sugar for dusting**

Preheat oven to 350 degrees and butter, or spray lightly with cooking oil, a 3 to 4-quart oven-proof casserole dish.

Using a fork, put holes in 2 or 3 places around each potato. Microwave on high until tender (this can be done in advance), approximately 12 minutes. Scrape potato out of skin into a food processor, or blender.

While potatoes are still warm, add water and process in blender, or food processor. Add sugars, baking powder, salt, cinnamon, flour, and vanilla extract. Add eggs one at a time, blending very well and adding softened butter as you blend.

Bake in oven for 45-60 minutes, until top is light golden brown and/or knife inserted about 1-inch from inside of casserole comes out clean. Remove from oven, sprinkle with confectioner's sugar and allow to sit at least 15 minutes, before serving. Does not require refrigeration.

Serve with Dessert Praline Topping or whipped cream.

Spinach Artichoke Dip

Finally - a delicious dip that isn't weighed down by cheese. If you are looking for a great dip for a party or for your own "quiet time", this is it!

SERVES 4-6

2	**bags frozen, chopped spinach (in a bag – not box)**
2	**(14-ounce) can artichoke hearts or bottoms, chopped**
½	**small white or red onion, finely minced**
1	**teaspoon minced garlic**
1-1½	**cup finely shredded Mozzarella cheese**
1	**cup (or more) real mayonnaise or ½ cup mayonnaise and ½ cup sour cream, if preferred**
½	**teaspoon yellow or Dijon mustard**
	salt and pepper
1	**fresh plum tomato, diced**
	grated Parmesan cheese, optional
	salt and pepper to taste

Rinse frozen spinach in a colander and squeeze out water. Using a paper towel, remove excess moisture. Chop spinach if not already cut. Put spinach in a large microwaveable bowl.

Rinse artichokes and dry with paper towel, then chop, and add to spinach.

Add onion, garlic, cheese, mayonnaise, and mustard. Stir well. Add salt and pepper to taste. If mixture is a little dry, add mayonnaise one tablespoon at a time until it is smooth. Heat in microwave until hot throughout, stirring at least once during heating process. Bottom of bowl will be very hot when ready. Stir again and place in a serving dish.

Season with salt and pepper. Garnish with diced fresh plum tomato and a sprinkling of grated Parmesan cheese if desired.

Serve warm with chips.

Irresistibly Italian American

Mama Mia, we can never get enough of your pasta...

Contents

-----Irresistibly Italian American-----

Alfredo Sauce

-----Irresistibly Italian American-----

Fresh alfredo sauce is great with a variety of sautéed or roasted vegetables, chicken or seafood.

SERVES 4

1   tablespoon olive oil

1   clove garlic, peeled and sliced very thin

¼   teaspoon Kosher salt

¼   teaspoon white pepper

½   cup (1 stick), plus 2 tablespoons unsalted butter

1   pint (16 ounces) whipping cream

1   cup fresh Parmesan cheese, grated

1   teaspoon minced fresh, or ¼ teaspoon dried, parsley

pasta noodles, your choice

In a 10-inch skillet, heat oil then sauté garlic for 2 minutes. Add salt, pepper and butter and stir until butter is melted. Add cream and bring to a simmer. Remove from heat and stir in cheese and parsley. Stir until sauce is smooth, using a whisk if necessary.

Toss with cooked noodles of choice and serve warm.

Italian Meat Sauce

-----Irresistibly Italian American-----

Use chuck roast, chicken or pork, browned and cooked like ribs, with seasonings. Or, do a combination of these and add browned ground meat. Make sauce a day in advance to allow fat to be skimmed and flavors to blend.

SERVES 6-8

6-8	long beef ribs
4	marrowbones, meatballs, and/or Italian sausage, optional
1	teaspoon garlic powder
1	teaspoon pepper
1	teaspoon salt
4	cups hot water
1	large onion, chopped
1	tablespoon minced garlic
2	tablespoons olive oil
1	(12-ounce) can Contadina tomato paste
1	(28-ounce) can crushed tomatoes
1	teaspoon dried parsley
8	ounces sliced mushrooms, sauteed
1	(2.5-ounce) can black olives, drained, rinsed and sliced
1	large onion, sliced into rings

MEAT PREPARATION

Preheat oven to 425 degrees. Season beef ribs with garlic powder, pepper, and salt. Put ribs (and marrowbones) on rack sprayed with cooking oil and brown both sides of ribs in oven, 30-60 minutes. Put the hot water into a large pot and bring to a boil. When ribs are brown, combine the ribs and the pan drippings in the pot of hot water with the onion and minced garlic. Simmer with lid on at least one hour. Take the ribs out of the stock and cool them on the rack. Once they have cooled, take the fat off the ribs and the bone. Chop the meat in bite size pieces and add meat back to stock.

SAUCE PREPARATION

In a large skillet, heat olive oil. Put the tomato paste in skillet and fry it, stirring constantly. Do not scrape the bottom of the pan while you are stirring. The paste is done when it changes color to a darker red and begins to curdle. Add fried paste to beef stock and crushed tomatoes and stir well. Add parsley, sautéed sliced mushrooms, sliced black olives and onion and simmer with lid on (or almost on) until it tastes yummy – adjust seasonings (salt and pepper) as needed.

Meaty Marinara Sauce

-----Irresistibly Italian American-----

Oh my mama - for me she cooks the greatest flavors - the aroma wafting through the kitchen draws you to the meal like a moth to a flame.

SERVES 6-8

¼	**cup olive oil**
1	**pound ground chuck or sirloin (chuck provides more meat flavor)**
1	**large yellow onion, diced chunky**
½	**pound mushrooms, sliced, optional**
1	**teaspoon Kosher salt**
½	**tablespoon ground black pepper or red pepper flakes**
1-2	**tablespoons minced garlic**
2	**teaspoons dry parsley**
2	**teaspoons beef granules**
2	**cups water**
1	**(28-ounce) can crushed tomatoes**
1	**(2.5-ounce) can sliced black olives, drained, optional**

Heat olive oil in a 6-quart or larger Dutch oven to medium high.

Add ground meat and begin to sauté. Stir meat and add onion, then mushrooms and sauté until meat loses pink color and vegetables wilt.

Add salt, pepper, garlic and parsley and sauté a few more minutes, stirring often.

Add beef granules, water, crushed tomatoes and black olives, cover and bring to a slow boil.

Simmer ½-1 hour, stirring often to keep sauce from sticking. Adjust seasonings according to taste. If you prefer more meat flavor, add beef granules, ¼ teaspoon at a time until you reach desired taste.

Sauce may be used immediately. or made a day in advance and refrigerated thus allowing flavors to blend and bloom.

Red Gravy

-----Irresistibly Italian American-----

Want taste with ease of preparation? This is the one for you. Yummy flavor without much effort.

SERVES 3-4

¼	cup olive oil
1	small onion, chopped
1	teaspoon minced garlic
1	(28-ounce) can plus 7-ounces can crushed tomatoes
1	cup hot water, or chicken or beef broth
1	teaspoon fresh or ¼ teaspoon dried parsley
1	bay leaf
½	teaspoon salt
½	teaspoon crushed red pepper flakes
1	teaspoon minced fresh, or ¼ teaspoon dried, basil, optional

In a 3-quart or larger saucepan, heat oil over medium heat. Add onions and sauté for 5-6 minutes; add garlic the last minute.

Add tomatoes and remaining ingredients and bring to a boil. Lower the heat so the sauce is at a high simmer and cook, stirring frequently until thickened, about 45 minutes. Remove bay leaf, taste and adjust seasonings if necessary.

Shrimp in Light Cream Sauce

-----Irresistibly Italian American-----

Crawfish, scallops or crab meat can be substituted for shrimp. If using cooked lump crab meat, do not sauté crab, wait and gently blend it into sauce just before serving.

SERVES 3-4

2	**tablespoons butter**
1	**tablespoon light olive or canola oil**
1	**pound raw, frozen and defrosted shelled and de-veined large shrimp**
½	**teaspoon cayenne or crushed red pepper flakes**
3	**tablespoons raw onion, minced**
1	**teaspoon minced garlic**
½	**(10-ounce) can Rotel tomatoes, well drained**
¼	**teaspoon celery seed**
8	**ounces heavy whipping cream**
½	**cup grated parmesan cheese**
1	**teaspoon coarse ground black pepper**
1	**pound warm al dente pasta**
¼	**cup minced fresh parsley**
½	**cup toasted pine nuts, optional**

Melt butter with oil in 2½-quart non-stick saucepan. Add shrimp or other seafood with pepper and sauté until lightly brown on both sides. Add onion and garlic and stir well. Remove shrimp and its seasonings to a bowl and set aside.

Put Rotel tomatoes and celery seed into the saucepan and stir well, scraping brown bits from bottom of pan. Add heavy whipping cream. Simmer at a medium boil until sauce thickens and is slightly reduced, no more than 5 minutes. Add cheese and stir until dissolved. Add shrimp and other seasonings from bowl and stir until well blended. Bring to a low boil and simmer on medium for about 3-4 minutes while stirring constantly.

Mix a small amount of sauce into warm al dente pasta of choice. Top each serving with a generous portion of sauce with seafood and tomatoes and sprinkle a small amount of parsley and pine nuts, on top.

Italian American Poached Eggs

-----Irresistibly Italian American-----

Do not miss this! In our family we consider eggs cooked in the suga to be a delicacy. It is simple to prepare and you have to cook more than one per person because you will have everyone wishing for more.

Makes 1-2 eggs per person

1	**cup suga, marinara sauce or canned tomato sauce**
½	**cup water**
2-8	**eggs**

Spray with oil or grease a deep, 9 to 10-inch skillet, and heat over medium high heat. Add sauce and water and reduce heat to medium. Bring to slight simmer (no boiling action).

Break eggs, one at a time, into a small custard bowl or cup, then gently pour egg into hot liquid until all eggs are in sauce. When eggs begin to set (lose liquidity), about 5 minutes, you can gently turn eggs over. Try not to break the yolks and do not turn more than once. Cook eggs until yolk appears well done – 10 minutes or more. Season to taste with salt and pepper.

Do not stir, just slide into a small serving dish and serve immediately as is.

If you are not planning to serve immediately, turn heat off. When ready to serve add a couple of tablespoons of water and re-heat. When sauce reaches a simmer, turn burner off.

Suga ~ Slow Cooked Tomato Gravy

-----Irresistibly Italian American-----

Truly a gladiator of tomato sauces - a winner every time. For a special treat at our house we simply get a bowl of gravy sauce and dip crusty bread in it. Yum!

Makes 10-12 cups

	10-inch, 8-quart or larger heavy saucepan or Dutch oven with cover
½	**cup olive oil**
1	**large onion, minced**
1	**tablespoon minced garlic**
1	**(6-ounce) can tomato paste**
1	**tablespoon minced fresh parsley**
½	**teaspoon red pepper flakes, more as needed**
½	**teaspoon salt, more as needed**
1	**(28-30 ounce) can crushed tomatoes**
8	**cups hot water or broth (chicken or beef)**

Spray or grease a large saucepan, add about 2 tablespoons of oil and heat over medium-high heat. Add onions and sauté for 3-4 minutes, stirring frequently.

Push onions to side of skillet and add garlic. Lower the heat to medium-low and cook garlic for one minute then mix in with onions and continue to sauté and stir for another several minutes, being careful not to brown garlic (burned garlic is bitter).

Add the remaining oil to pan, turn heat to medium. Push onions and garlic to the side and add tomato paste. Cook for a minute then mix in parsley, red pepper and salt and cook another couple of minutes, stirring all (including onions and garlic) constantly. Add crushed tomatoes and stir well. Add about 2 cups of the hot water or broth and stir again.

Turn heat to high, bring to a quick boil and then simmer over medium heat for 5-6 minutes, stirring constantly. Keep sauce from sticking to bottom of pot by scraping bottom as you stir. Add remaining liquid and bring to a high boil.

Turn heat to medium low when boiling begins; maintain a steady gentle boil. Note the liquid level in the pot – you do not want your finished sauce to be any lower. Cover with lid and cook at least an hour before checking again. After an hour, remove lid, stir well, and add more liquid if necessary. Cover, but leave a space for steam to escape. Continue to cook for several hours, checking periodically and adding liquid as necessary. Taste and adjust salt and pepper to taste.

Serve with pasta, meat with vegetables, in lasagna, on fried eggplant and other Italian dishes.

Chicken Breast Delizioso

-----*Irresistibly Italian American*-----

This dish is excellent with a side of fried eggplant, or pasta of choice tossed with warm extra virgin olive oil, minced fresh parsley or basil, kosher salt and crushed red pepper flakes.

SERVES 4

2	**large egg whites, lightly beaten with 1 tablespoon water**
	Kosher salt and crushed red pepper flakes, to taste
1	**clove garlic (1 tablespoon), smashed and minced fine**
1	**cup all-purpose flour seasoned with ½ teaspoon each salt and pepper**
4	**large boneless chicken breasts**
2	**cups dry Italian seasoned bread crumbs**
1	**teaspoon lemon pepper seasoning (mix with bread crumbs)**
	cooking spray oil
¼	**cup vegetable oil plus 2 tablespoons olive oil**
4	**cups baby spinach, washed and dried**
6	**ounces fresh Mozzarella cheese balls or block cut in ¼-inch cubes or smaller**
2-3	**tablespoons olive oil**
1	**cup tomatoes, chopped, or cherry tomatoes halved**
2	**tablespoons red wine or balsamic vinegar**

Prepare everything in advance, including breading chicken and readying salad ingredients. Thirty minutes before you are ready to serve, preheat oven to 400 degrees.

Mix beaten eggs, a pinch of salt and pepper, and minced garlic in a bowl and set aside. Lightly season flour with salt and pepper and put into zip-lock bag or on plate. Wrap each breast loosely in clear plastic wrap and place on top of paper towel on a cutting board. Pound lightly until knots are removed from chicken breast then lightly season each breast with salt and pepper.

Using the assembly line method, dust each breast with flour, then dip in egg mixture. Press into bread crumbs mixed with lemon pepper seasoning, to make sure crumbs adhere. Set aside. (Remaining bread crumbs and flour can be frozen in separate plastic bags for later use.) If you prefer a crispier coating, assemble ingredients in advance but do the breading immediately before sautéing.

Spray or grease a large 10-inch skillet, with vegetable oil. Add the vegetable and olive oil combination to the skillet and heat over medium heat until hot but not smoking. Sauté breasts about 6 minutes, turning once, until golden on both sides. Transfer to a large glass baking dish coated with oil, and bake in preheated oven until done, about 8 minutes.

While chicken is baking, toss salad greens and Mozzarella with olive oil, salt and pepper. Add tomatoes and vinegar and toss again. Add more salt or pepper to taste and toss lightly.

When chicken is done, transfer to four serving plates. Top each breast with ¼ of salad; heat will slightly wilt greens and warm cheese. Serve immediately.

Make mealtime a happy time in your home - *Good meals are a balm for the body as well as the soul. Set the mood by preparing yourself. Allow all the problems and challenges of the day to fall away and just "be" for this time. Put a smile on your face that says "I am so happy to see you and spend time with you." Little gestures like greeting your partner or children with a hug or kiss as they come to the table go a long way to opening the door to great interaction. In our house everyone gives a little kiss to the person on each side of them right after saying Grace before meals. Isn't that nice, dessert first with no extra calories!!*

Italian Sausage and Peppers

-----Irresistibly Italian American-----

An American favorite - it is a robust combination of rich flavors that satisfy and comfort.

SERVES 4

4	**links sweet Italian sausage**
	water, as needed
¼	**cup olive oil, or as needed**
4	**medium bell peppers, 2 green and 2 yellow, seeded and cut in 1-inch strips**
1	**small red or white onion, peeled and cut in ½-inch strips**
1	**teaspoon minced garlic, or 2 cloves peeled and sliced thin**
12	**small cherry tomatoes, rinsed and dried**
½	**cup chicken broth**
1	**teaspoon red pepper flakes**
	salt and pepper to taste

Perforate the sausages all over with a fork. Put sausages in a microwaveable casserole dish, cover with water and cook for about 10 minutes on high power. Remove from microwave and drain all liquid. Cut sausages on the diagonal into bite size pieces. Set aside.

In a large, heavy skillet, heat oil until hot but not smoking. Add the peppers and onions to the skillet and cook, stirring frequently, for about 5 minutes. Add sausage, garlic, and cherry tomatoes and fry another 3 minutes, then add chicken broth and red pepper flakes, cover and simmer 5 minutes, or until no pink remains in sausage. Add salt and pepper to taste.

Serve as a side dish or over hot pasta.

Cook together - *If children are old enough, introduce them to the kitchen and the joys of creating something the family will enjoy. The positive affirmations they will receive for their contribution will help develop self-esteem, responsibility, fond memories and a sense of family for life.*

Meatballs

When you have some time on your hands you may choose to make one or more recipes of meatballs and freeze them for later use. They hold well in the freezer for several months in an airtight container.

SERVES 4-6

1	**pound hamburger, chuck or sirloin, the better the cut the better the taste**
¼	**cup bread crumbs, Italian, garlic herb, or plain**
1	**large or 2 small egg(s), slightly beaten**
2-4	**tablespoons water or tomato sauce**
1	**teaspoon garlic powder**
½	**teaspoon dried parsley flakes**
	salt and pepper to taste
¼	**cup Parmesan cheese, grated, optional**
	cooking oil for frying

Put all ingredients, except oil, in a large bowl and mix by hand, adding a little water if too dry. You do not want the meatballs too moist or they will fall apart, so add liquid sparingly.

Lay out a pan or foil on which to put shaped meatballs. Shape meat balls into your favorite size and place on foil/pan. (The size of a golf ball is standard for large and cherry tomato for small). Greasing your hands or gloves helps in working with the meatballs. Add an inch of oil to a deep 10-inch frying pan. Heat to hot but not smoking, over medium high heat. Flatten the meatball a little so it is easy to keep in place in skillet.

Carefully add meatballs to pan and fry until brown, turning only once. Meatballs need to have a good brown on them, though not a crust, so they will hold together when placed in a sauce. After frying meatballs, place them on a layer of paper towels to absorb excess oil.

Use now or freeze for later use.

Artichoke and Pasta Alfredo

-----Irresistibly Italian American-----

For a delicious touch, peel and de-vein ½ pound large raw shrimp and add to skillet with artichoke hearts sautéing only until shrimp become opaque.

SERVES 4

2	**(14-ounce) cans artichoke hearts**
½	**cup (1 stick), unsalted butter, softened**
3	**tablespoons olive oil**
1½	**(12-ounces) cups vermicelli spaghetti or bowtie pasta**
1	**tablespoon minced garlic**
1	**pint (16 ounces) whipping cream**
1	**teaspoon minced fresh, or ¼ teaspoon dried, parsley**
1	**cup fresh Parmesan Cheese, grated, or ¾ cup dried grated parmesan**
½	**teaspoon Kosher salt**
½	**teaspoon crushed red pepper flakes**
¼	**cup Italian seasoned bread crumbs**

Rinse hearts carefully but thoroughly under running water, drain and dry between paper towels.

Melt the butter with 1 tablespoon oil over medium heat in a large, 10 to 12-inch skillet. When butter begins to bubble around the edges, lay hearts in a single layer and roll to coat them.

Cover pan and let hearts steam for about 3 minutes, more if needed to lightly brown.

While artichokes are cooking, put vermicelli or bowtie to boil in a large pot of salted water, according to package directions. Cook until al dente. Drain in a colander and toss with remaining olive oil.

When artichokes have cooked, uncover skillet and raise heat to medium-high. Add garlic and cook another 1-2 minutes. Gently remove the artichokes and keep warm until sauce is finished.

Stir cream and parsley into skillet, stirring constantly, and simmer for about 3 minutes.

Remove skillet from heat and stir in cheese, salt and pepper until smooth. Taste and adjust seasonings. Add the hearts and pasta and toss. Transfer contents to a serving dish, sprinkle bread crumbs and serve.

Castroville, California, the "Artichoke Capital of the World" celebrates the artichoke and crowns a queen at the annual festival. A young Hollywood starlet was making a publicity tour around the state when she visited Castroville's first festival. She was such a hit they gave her the crown and that was how Marilyn Monroe became the first Artichoke Queen of the World.

Everyone's favorite picnic - *Turn meal time into fun time and great memories - Cruise the aisles of your supermarket and load your cart with whatever delights you can find – things you would not ordinarily let your children eat – and set out a picnic with a blanket on the living room floor or on a table in the backyard, weather permitting. Fix their favorite foods like fried chicken and potato salad and let them go at it. Be sure to smile and laugh a lot. Make this a paper plates and no utensils needed affair – it's a picnic. Provide scoop shaped chips with which to eat potato salad and baked beans, eat green salad and chicken with fingers, chill soft drinks in their favorite flavors. And, of course, make their favorite dessert, cookies or whatever – maybe have 'make your own sundae" ice cream sundaes. Be sure to provide a large roll of paper towels or loads of paper napkins. A nice addition would be lemon halves to squeeze for cleaning hands – or a bottle of Purell hand cleaner to pass around. The object of this meal is to enjoy yourselves together – it is a great bonding experience. Take lots of pictures of everyone having a great time. Your kids will think you are the "coolest."*

Asparagus and Shrimp with Pasta

-----Irresistibly Italian American-----

A delicious departure from steamed asparagus and elegant in its own right, this will be a favorite of asparagus lovers.

SERVES 4-6

3	tablespoons extra-virgin olive oil
1	pound asparagus, trimmed and cut (on the diagonal) into ¼-inch pieces
1	teaspoon salt
2	tablespoons red onion, minced
2	cloves garlic, minced
1	tablespoon unsalted butter
18	jumbo shrimp, peeled and de-veined
½	teaspoon red pepper flakes
6	small plum tomatoes, diced
½	cup chicken broth
6	stuffed green or pitted black olives, drained well
1½	cup (12-ounces) small shell or elbow macaroni
½	cup finely fresh Mozzarella or Parmesan cheese, shredded
3	tablespoons fresh cilantro, chopped

Spray or coat a large skillet with oil. Heat 2 tablespoons olive oil, over medium-high heat, until hot but not smoking. Add asparagus and ¼ teaspoon salt, cover and cook 2 minutes. Add onions and garlic and sauté another 2 minutes. Remove asparagus to a plate.

Set burner on high; heat the remaining tablespoon olive oil and butter in same skillet. Add shrimp, sprinkle with pepper flakes, and sauté uncovered one minute on each side until golden. Add tomatoes and broth and simmer until shrimp are just opaque in center, 2 to 3 minutes. Remove pan from heat and stir in asparagus and olives. Taste and adjust seasonings as necessary.

Cook pasta in an 8-quart saucepan according to package directions, until tender but firm (al dente). Drain. Do not rinse.

Toss pasta with asparagus and shrimp sauce, sprinkle lightly with cheese and cilantro and serve immediately.

Love Me Tender Lasagna

-----Irresistibly Italian American-----

A dish of homemade lasagna, a jug of wine and thou is a true Italian love potion - it engenders awe and delight as no other food can. All you need is a salad to complete the meal.

SERVES 8-10

10 x 14 x 2½-inch, lasagna baking dish

3   **cups Ricotta filling recipe, made in advance and refrigerated**

10   **ounces lasagna noodles**

7   **cups Italian meat sauce recipe, warmed**

1½-2 pounds mozzarella cheese, sliced very thin (or 40 ounces finely shredded)

ground black pepper

¼   **cup Parmesan or Romano cheese, grated**

Grease a large lasagna baking dish with olive oil.

Remove ricotta from refrigerator and bring to room temperature while noodles are cooking.

Cook noodles, according to package directions, until slightly tender. Drain in large colander.

Spoon a thin layer of meat sauce (about 1½ cups) into bottom of baking dish. Layer noodles to completely cover bottom of dish. This may take four noodles. If using a 9 x 13-inch pan the quantities will be less. Put another layer over the seams, 3 to 4 more noodles. Over noodles, carefully spread half the ricotta filling. Cover with a single layer of sliced mozzarella or 2 cups (16-ounces) shredded mozzarella. Cover with meat sauce (about 2 cups). Lightly season layer with black pepper. Repeat layering.

Put remaining noodles (about 4) in a layer on top. Spread remaining sauce over noodles. Sprinkle Parmesan cheese and 1 cup mozzarella.

Bake lasagna at 375 degrees for 35-40 minutes until bubbling and beginning to brown. Remove and let stand at least 10 minutes. Lasagna may be assembled and refrigerated. It can be frozen for several months. Allow an additional 15 minutes or more in the oven if chilled.

Meatballs and Spaghetti

-----Irresistibly Italian American-----

How we all love this traditional dish - and this is a particularly good recipe with flavorful and delicious meatballs in a heavenly sauce.

SERVES 4-6

1   **recipe Meatballs**

1   **recipe Suga-Slow Cooked Tomato Gravy**

1   **pound spaghetti, vermicelli or other favorite**

If meatballs or gravy sauce have been prepared in advance, heat sauce to boiling in a 6-quart saucepan. Add meatballs and bring to a boil. Turn fire low enough to maintain sauce at a bubbling boil. Cook meatballs in sauce one hour if frozen, 45 minutes if not frozen. When meatballs are fully cooked, turn off the heat. Let meatballs sit in sauce to absorb the flavor while you prepare the spaghetti.

If you prefer a thicker sauce, remove meatballs, set aside and keep warm. Return to a boil, reduce heat to medium-high and cook sauce at a medium boil, uncovered, until it thickens to the consistency you like. Taste the sauce while it is reducing and adjust salt and other seasonings according to your preference.

While the sauce is reducing, fill a large 6-quart pot about ⅔ full of water. Bring to a boil and cook spaghetti or pasta to al dente according to package directions. Drain spaghetti thoroughly, return to cooking pot and toss with ¼ cup or more sauce to keep it from sticking together as it cools. Put spaghetti in a serving bowl, surround with meatballs and sauce.

Pasta Side Dish

-----Irresistibly Italian American-----

A quick and tasty complement to meat and fish dishes to enhance your meal.

SERVES 2-3

12	**ounces fettuccini noodles**
2	**tablespoons garlic, finely minced or thinly sliced**
1	**tablespoon melted butter**
¼	**cup parsley, chopped - fresh is best**
¼	**cup fresh Parmesan cheese, grated**
2	**tablespoons olive oil**
1	**teaspoon lemon pepper seasoning, optional**
¼	**teaspoon red pepper flakes**

Cook fettuccini in boiling salted water according to package directions; drain well.

Lightly saute garlic in butter for about 1-2 minutes.

Combine remaining ingredients in a large bowl. Add hot pasta and garlic butter and toss to coat.

Serve immediately with meat dish of choice.

Pasta with Peas

-----Irresistibly Italian American-----

A very healthy recipe sure to delight sweet pea lovers as well as many others.

SERVES 4-6

1½	**(12-ounces) cups medium elbow macaroni**
1	**(8-ounces) cup small white boiler onions**
2	**cloves garlic, peeled and crushed or thinly sliced**
2/3	**cup olive oil**
1	**(8-ounces) cup sliced fresh mushrooms**
2	**(16-ounces) cup frozen green peas**
1+	**(8–10 ounces) cup chicken or vegetable stock**
2	**(16-ounces) cup canned, diced tomatoes**
¼	**teaspoon crushed red pepper flakes**
½	**teaspoon black pepper**
1	**teaspoon salt, or to taste**
1	**teaspoon fresh parsley, chopped**
	grated Parmesan or Mozzarella cheese, optional
	crusty garlic bread

Heat large pot of water for macaroni. Cut ends off onions and peel, leaving whole. Peel and crush garlic or thinly slice.

In a deep skillet, put ½ cup of the oil and bring to medium high heat. Add fresh mushrooms and onions and sauté until slightly caramelized. Add garlic and sauté for 1 minute to release flavor. Add peas and sauté 1 minute. When heated through, add ½ the stock, turn heat to medium and cook until peas soften, 5 minutes.

Bring water in large pot to boil and add macaroni. Bring to a boil, turn heat to medium and cook until al dente.

To vegetables, add remaining stock, tomatoes crushed by hand as you add them, red and black pepper, and salt. Simmer until peas are barely tender. Allow to sit over lowest possible heat until macaroni has finished cooking.

Drain macaroni and add to vegetables. Toss and adjust seasonings. Sprinkle remaining oil and chopped parsley over dish. A sprinkling of grated Parmesan or Mozzarella cheese may also be added. Let sit 10 minutes for flavors to blend.

Serve with crusty garlic bread.

Rigoletto's Favorite Ricotta Filling

-----Irresistibly Italian American-----

The secret to savory lasagna is a good ricotta. For those who have not liked ricotta previously - you gotta try it - it will win you over!
It's good enough to eat alone.

SERVES ONE LASAGNA

2	**cups Ricotta cheese, drained**
¼	**cup Parmesan cheese**
1	**cup Mozzarella cheese, shredded**
1	**tablespoon parsley flakes**
1	**tablespoon minced garlic**
½	**teaspoon ground black pepper**
1	**teaspoons salt**
2	**beaten eggs**

Put all ingredients in a large bowl and mix well. May be used immediately or refrigerated overnight or frozen for later use.

Use ricotta filling in lasagna, to stuff pasta shells or manicotti or layer with penne pasta and tomato sauce in a casserole.

Assign conversation starter privileges - *If the evening meal has become a "pass the salt, please" ritual. You might spice up the meal by asking each member of the family to introduce a topic of conversation on a rotating basis. It can be something that happened during the day, a subject in school, a current event or a burning question. Obviously some topics are not appropriate for dinner conversation, but family rules will soon sort that out. Some families have each member drop a slip of paper in a container with their subject and then a drawing made at the table. The subject selected is the topic of conversation.*

Fried Potatoes and Eggs

-----Irresistibly Italian American-----

I remember this from my childhood - it is great in place of hash browns. A true comfort food - delicious and satisfying.

SERVES 4

2	**large red potatoes (about 1 pound)**
4	**large eggs**
½	**teaspoon salt, Kosher preferred**
½	**teaspoon ground black pepper**
1	**small onion, cut in half and sliced in thin slices**
½	**cup olive or vegetable oil**

Peel the potatoes and cut into ¼-inch thick circles.

Break eggs into a small bowl, add ½ teaspoon each salt and pepper and whisk until well blended. Set bowl of eggs aside.

Heat oil in a large skillet and heat on high until hot but not smoking. Turn heat down to medium-high, add potatoes and fry until they begin to brown. Turn potatoes over, add onions and gently mix them with the potatoes. Continue to fry until second side of potatoes is brown and onions are tender, a total of about 6-minutes frying.

Drain all but about 1-2 teaspoons of oil from skillet, pour eggs over all and mix well. Return to medium heat and cook until the texture is to your liking. Adjust seasonings.

Serve warm to hot.

Variation: Substitute 3-4 bell peppers for potatoes and delete onion

Red Potatoes Italiano

-----Irresistibly Italian American-----

Highlights the natural flavor to perfection. Leftovers are great for breakfast scrambled with eggs.

SERVES 4-6

6-8	**medium red potatoes, scrubbed and cut in eighths**
1	**large red or white onion, peeled and chunky cut**
3	**tablespoons extra virgin olive oil**
1	**teaspoon salt, Kosher preferred**
3	**tablespoons real bacon bits or diced prosciutto**
1	**tablespoon minced garlic or 6 large cloves sliced, optional**
½-1	**teaspoon ground pepper, pepperoncini if available**
3	**tablespoons butter, melted**
¼	**cup finely chopped cut parsley, or equivalent dried**
½	**cup Italian bread crumbs**
½	**cup shredded Mozzarella cheese**

Spray a large oven proof baking dish with cooking spray and preheat oven to 450 degrees.

In a large bowl, combine potatoes and onion and toss with olive oil. Salt and toss again. Put this in baking dish with cut side down, and bake for about 30 minutes.

Remove dish from oven, add bacon, garlic, and pepperoncini, and toss with partially cooked potatoes. Put another cut side of potatoes face down. Return dish to oven and bake an additional 10 minutes or more, until garlic is cooked and potatoes are tender.

Melt butter and add parsley. Remove vegetables from oven, drizzle parsley butter over all and toss. Sprinkle bread crumbs over all, and toss. Sprinkle cheese over all and return to oven just long enough to melt cheese. Serve warm.

Variation: If you don't like garlic or onions, leave them out. Experiment and perhaps substitute a cup of mushrooms or onion powder for ingredients you don't want.

Artichoke Green Beans

-----Irresistibly Italian American-----

Love stuffed artichokes but hate the work of preparation? This simple recipe provides all the distinct flavor of Italian Stuffed Artichokes with a minimum of effort and no taste of plain green beans.

SERVES 4-6

3	**(16-ounce) cans cut green beans, drained**
¼	**cup olive oil**
½	**teaspoon lemon pepper**
½	**teaspoon salt**
I	**cup bread crumbs**
½	**teaspoon garlic powder**
½	**teaspoon pepper**
2	**tablespoons dried parsley**
½	**cup Parmesan cheese, grated**
1	**(16-ounce) can drained artichoke hearts quarters, optional**

Preheat oven to 350 degrees.

Drain canned green beans in a colander, drizzle with olive oil and then toss well.

Place beans in a large bowl and sprinkle with lemon pepper, salt and mixture of bread crumbs, garlic, pepper, parsley and Parmesan cheese. Add artichoke hearts and toss.

Put mixture in an 11 x 13-inch pan or an oven proof casserole dish coated with oil. Sprinkle the remaining bread crumbs (the ones that did not adhere to the beans) to the top of the dish.

Bake for 30 minutes.

Easy table decorations even little ones can do - *Every once in a while, when setting the table, put out candles. Let smaller children light them before the meal (under supervision of course) and put them out at the end of the meal. Candles can be used for romantic meals as well, when two of you want to make a meal special. Or scatter small flowers or rose petals on the table for a nice touch – children can do this easily if you are not a perfectionist.*

Roasted Vegetables

-----Irresistibly Italian American-----

There is nothing quite like roasted food to highlight the natural flavors and perk up the palate.

SERVES 8

3	slices bacon cut in ½-inch strips, thick sliced works best
2	tablespoons extra-virgin olive oil
1	pound button mushrooms, cleaned and cut
1½	pound fresh green beans, rinsed and trimmed, may be broken in half
½	cup white or red onion, chunky sliced , optional
1	teaspoon ground white or black pepper
1	tablespoons minced garlic
½	cup fresh parsley, finely chopped
1	teaspoon Kosher salt

Preheat oven to 450 degrees.

Cook bacon crispy and drain. Set bacon aside. Put 2 tablespoons of the bacon grease with the 2 tablespoons olive oil. Cut larger mushrooms in half to make similar sized pieces. Put mushrooms, green beans, and onion in a large bowl and toss with olive oil and bacon grease mixture. Sprinkle pepper over all and toss again. Transfer mixture to a lightly greased 10 x 15-inch oven proof baking dish and roast on the center rack in preheated oven for 10 minutes.

After the vegetables have roasted 10 minutes, sprinkle with garlic, parsley, salt and stir. Roast until vegetables are tender and very lightly browned, about 10 minutes more. Eat crispy bacon while vegetables are cooking, or break it up and add as a topping.

Adjust seasonings if necessary.

Bean and Meatball Soup Italiano

-----Irresistibly Italian American-----

Warms your heart and satisfies your soul.

SERVES 8-10

3	tablespoons cooking oil (you can use the oil from frying meatballs)
1½	cups onion, diced, fresh or frozen
½	cup celery, chopped
1½	cups carrot, thin sticks or diced
2	tablespoons minced garlic
6	cups (49.5 ounces) chicken broth
3	cups water
½	cup thin sliced zucchini squash
2-3	cups small browned meatballs, fresh made or frozen (see Meatball recipe)
1	bay leaf
½	tablespoon minced parsley
1	cup uncooked small bowtie macaroni
2	cups canned or fresh cooked navy or northern beans, drained and rinsed
2	teaspoons salt
1	teaspoon crushed red pepper flakes
1	bag fresh baby spinach, washed

Heat oil in a large soup pot over high heat until it sizzles. Add onions and celery and sauté 5 minutes. Add carrots and garlic and bring to a sizzle; if needed, add a little chicken broth to continue sautéing. Lower heat and cook until onions begin to brown and carrots begin to soften, about 4-5 minutes.

Add broth and water, zucchini, meatballs, bay leaf, parsley, pasta, beans, salt and pepper. Bring to a boil, then cook uncovered at medium boil for 15 minutes or until pasta is al dente, stirring often. Stir in spinach and cook for about 5 minutes. Adjust seasonings as necessary and remove bay leaf.

Serve hot with a sprinkling of Italian cheese of choice on top.

Roasted Garlic and Olive Oil Dip

-----Irresistibly Italian American-----

Drizzle garlic olive oil mixture over steamed artichoke leaves, then sprinkle Parmeson cheese and Italian flavored bread crumbs over all.

Makes ½ cup

2	large heads garlic (about 3 inches wide)
2	tablespoons unsalted butter, melted
⅓	cup olive oil, classic or extra virgin
¼	teaspoon turmeric
1	tablespoon fresh parsley, leaves only, finely minced
½	teaspoon Kosher salt
½	teaspoon red pepper flakes or coarse ground black pepper

With oven rack in middle position in oven, preheat oven to 425 degrees.

Cut top ½-inch of garlic heads, exposing cloves. Leave the outside garlic papery skin on and discard tops. Use a large garlic cooker, or place garlic in a shallow pan or pie plate. Mix together remaining ingredients and pour over garlic heads. If using garlic cooker, place lid on top. When using a pan or plate, cover tightly with heavy duty aluminum foil and roast until garlic is golden and tender, a minimum of 1 to 1 ¼ hours. DO NOT OVER COOK – GARLIC WILL BURN. Do not open and check before 1 hour. After cooking, remove from oven, open foil and allow to sit at room temperature until cool enough to handle.

Using a fine-mesh sieve, strain oil into a 2-quart or larger bowl and discard bits left in sieve. When garlic is cool, squeeze soft garlic cloves into the bowl with the seasoned butter/oil and discard peel. Mash well with a fork until well blended and season to taste.

Use as a flavorful dip for crusty Italian bread or add 2 tablespoons more melted butter and drizzle on steamed artichoke leaves or over grilled vegetables.

Lip Smackin' Louisiana

Jambalaya, Crawfish Pie, all kinds of Gumbo...

Contents

-----Lip Smackin' Louisiana-----

The Origin of Gumbo

Originated in South Louisiana, the land of Zydeco and Voodoo Queen Marie Laveau, crawfish boils and boudin (a highly seasoned Cajun sausage made of pork, rice and spices). Gumbo is served daily up and down the coast of the Gulf of Mexico by Cajuns (descendants of *18th century French colonists exiled from Acadia, Nova Scotia*) and other residents alike.

The first French settlers in the state attempted to make their beloved Bouillabaisse, a highly seasoned fish stew, out of local ingredients. Okra seeds were brought over by the slaves from Africa and Cayenne was brought up by the Spanish from the Caribbean and South America. As the African Americans and Spanish in the area added a bit of this and a dash of that from their native cooking into the stew, it evolved into the spicy soup we know today as gumbo (originating from the Central African Bantu word for okra).

There are as many varieties of gumbo as there are combinations of chicken, duck, quail, andouille (cajun smoked sausage), and seafood such as crab, shrimp, and oysters fresh from the Gulf of Mexico.

Today, gumbo begins with a "roux" (flour and oil stirred over medium-high heat until it becomes a dark mahogany brown), and a broth or stock. Okra is added for thickening along with seasonings the locals refer to as "the trinity" (onion, celery and bell pepper), plus various other seasonings and combinations of meat or seafood, all slow simmered until the flavors are well blended.

In Louisiana, gumbo is served with freshly boiled or steamed white rice which is served separately with each bowl of gumbo, accompanied by saltine crackers and sometimes potato salad on the side. Gumbo is one of the dishes that supports the argument that Louisiana is the only place in the United States that developed a true Native American cuisine.

Roux

-----Lip Smackin' Louisiana-----

Roux is used in gumbo and often as a base for cream or water gravies.

Makes 1-1½ cups
2 cups water
⅓ cup all-purpose white flour
⅓ cup hot oil

Set aside two cups of water. In large skillet, add flour to hot oil (add more oil if necessary) and stir constantly until roux (flour oil mixture) becomes a very dark brown (mahogany color) without getting a burned look.

It is very important you keep the flour oil mixture moving constantly by scraping the bottom and sides of the skillet with a spatula.

When the flour is sufficiently brown, carefully add about ½ cup of the two cups water and stir constantly until the steam wears down. Then add the rest of the water. Addition of the water will cause a lot of steam so be careful not to get burned. Stir well, bring soup back to a boil, reduce heat to medium low and simmer for one hour.

Add roux to any hot seasoned stock to make various sauces and gravies.

Chicken and Sausage Gumbo

-----Lip Smackin' Louisiana-----

Fresh steamed white rice can be served with gumbo. Whether the gumbo is served over a mound of rice or rice is put into the gumbo is a discussion among purists. Try it both ways to determine your favorite technique.

SERVES 5-6

4	cups chicken broth
4	cups water
1	(14.5-ounce can petite diced tomatoes or 1 large fresh tomato chopped
½	cup chopped fresh curly parsley (not Italian or flat parsley)
½	teaspoon salt
¼-½	teaspoon ground red (cayenne) pepper
1	teaspoon ground black pepper
⅛	teaspoon turmeric
2	bay leaves
1	cup cooking oil
¼-1	cup chopped fresh or frozen raw okra
¾	cup chopped onion (1 small)
½	cup green bell pepper, seeded and chopped
2-3	cloves garlic smashed and sliced
1	small chicken, cut in pieces
	salt, pepper and garlic powder to dust chicken
1	cup flour seasoned with ½ teaspoon each salt, pepper, and garlic powder
1	pound Andouille or beef sausage links, cut in bite size pieces

Spray your pot with cooking oil spray and put broth and 2 cups of the water into the pot (reserving 2 cups water for diluting browned flour over high heat). Add tomatoes, parsley, salt, red and black pepper, turmeric, and bay leaves and bring to a boil. Cover pot, turn heat to low and simmer.

Put oil in a medium to large skillet and heat over high heat. When oil is hot but not smoking, turn heat to medium high, add okra, and fry until seeds in okra are cooked and beginning to brown. Cut up other ingredients while the okra is cooking. Remove okra from oil with a slotted spoon or spatula and add to simmering soup.

Add more oil if needed. Turn heat under skillet to high and add onion and green pepper; fry until beginning to brown. Add garlic and fry 30-45 seconds longer. Remove seasonings from oil with a slotted spoon and add to soup pot. Turn heat off under skillet.

Dust chicken pieces with salt, pepper, and garlic

powder. Put flour, salt, pepper and garlic powder in a bowl or large plastic zip bag and mix well. Put chicken pieces in all at once and mix with seasoned flour until pieces are coated.

Turn heat under skillet to medium high and heat until hot but not smoking. Fry chicken on all sides until lightly brown, set it aside on a plate lined with paper towels (to soak up extra grease) then fry sausage until lightly brown and put on the side with the chicken.

Pour oil from skillet into a Pyrex or metal measuring cup. Measure ¼ cup of the oil and return it to skillet over high heat. (Discard remaining oil when cooled.) Add ¼ cup of the remaining seasoned flour, taken from coating chicken, to the hot oil and stir constantly with a spatula until roux (flour oil mixture) becomes a rich, dark mahogany color and goes from a thin liquid to a thick consistency. **It is very important you keep the flour and oil mixture moving constantly by scraping the bottom and sides of the skillet with your spatula.**

When the flour is sufficiently brown, carefully add the remaining 2 cups hot water while stirring constantly. Addition of the water will cause a lot of steam so be careful not to get burned. After steaming has stopped and water is well mixed into browned flour, add roux to soup pot. Stir well, add browned chicken and sausage and bring gumbo back to a boil, reduce heat to medium low and simmer, covered, for 1 hour. Check gumbo after 30 minutes, it should be soupy but not watery. If too thick, add water a little at a time until it becomes a light cream consistency. Taste gumbo, remove bay leaves and adjust seasonings. Cook the remaining 30 minutes. While gumbo cooks, make steamed rice.

Shrimp Gumbo

-----Lip Smackin' Louisiana-----

In Cajun Country saltine crackers accompany the gumbo and potato salad is often the side dish of choice.

SERVES 4-6

2	**pounds headless medium fresh or frozen shrimp**
8	**cups water**
1	**cup petite diced canned tomatoes or 1 large fresh tomato chopped**
¼	**cup fresh curly parsley, chopped (not Italian or flat parsley), without stems**
½	**teaspoon celery seed or ½ cup chopped celery**
1	**teaspoon salt**
¼	**teaspoon ground red (cayenne) pepper, or more for a hotter soup**
1	**teaspoon black pepper**
⅛	**teaspoon turmeric**
1	**bay leaf**
½	**cup cooking oil**
½	**cup fresh or frozen raw okra, chopped**
1	**large sweet onion, chopped**
½	**cup green bell pepper, seeded and chopped**
2-3	**cloves garlic, smashed and sliced**
⅓	**cup all-purpose white flour**

Peel, de-vein shrimp and put them in a bowl of ice water. Refrigerate until ready to use. Keep shrimp shells separate.

Rinse shrimp shells and put them in a large pot with 6 cups of water and boil for 5 minutes over high heat.

Drain shells thoroughly and put hot stock into a 5-quart or larger soup pot over high heat. Discard shells. Add tomatoes, parsley, celery seeds, salt, red and black pepper, turmeric, and bay leaf to stock and bring to a boil. Turn flame to low and simmer.

Put oil in a medium to large skillet and heat over high heat. When oil is hot but not smoking turn heat to medium high, add okra, and fry until seeds in okra are cooked and beginning to brown. Remove okra from oil with a slotted spoon or spatula and add to simmering stock liquid. (You can transfer the okra to a plate lined with a paper towel first, to soak up some of the grease from the okra.)

Turn heat under skillet to high and add onion and green pepper; fry until beginning to brown. Add garlic and fry 30-45 seconds longer.

Remove seasonings from oil with a slotted spoon and add to simmering liquid. (As with the okra, you can soak up any excess grease from the mixture by putting it on a paper towel for a few minutes before adding to the liquid.)

Set aside two cups of water. Add flour to hot oil (add more oil if necessary) and stir constantly until roux (flour oil mixture) becomes a very dark brown (mahogany color) without getting a burned look. It is very important you keep the flour oil mixture moving constantly by scraping the bottom and sides of the skillet with a spatula.

When the flour is sufficiently brown, carefully add about ½ cup of the two cups water and stir constantly until the steam wears down. Then add the rest of the water. Addition of the water will cause a great deal of steam so be cautioned not to get burned. After steaming has stopped and water is well mixed into browned flour, add roux to simmering stock liquid. Stir well, bring soup back to a boil, reduce heat to medium low and simmer for 1 hour.

At this point, the soup should be tasty on its own and not strong on salt. Taste soup and adjust seasonings by adding salt and pepper a little at a time if necessary. Be careful not to over salt. Remove bay leaf. Remove shrimp from refrigerator, drain and add to stock liquid. Bring to a boil over high heat. Do not cover pot. Boil 10-15 minutes or until shrimp become opaque and turns pink. Remove from heat and let rest for at least 30 minutes for flavors to blend. Serve with steamed rice.

To reduce the fat content, refrigerate overnight and skim the grease before heating to serve.

Seafood Gumbo

Seafood gumbo uses the same recipe as Shrimp Gumbo, with a different variation of seafood. Vary seafood to tempt your tastebuds!

SERVES 4-6

Maximum of 3 pounds of a combination of 2 or more of the following –

1   **cup lump crab meat OR**

1   **pound shelled raw crab claw fingers (with one piece of shell left as a handle)**

      shrimp

      firm-flesh fish, skinned and cut in bite size pieces

8-10 ounces rinsed and drained raw oysters

      firm, flesh fish skinned and cut into bite sized pieces

Prepare soup as directed for shrimp gumbo.

If using crab claws, add those first and cook 10 minutes. Next add shrimp and/or fish to the soup and cook 10 minutes. Add oysters and or crab meat and cook another 5 minutes.

If using oysters, cut initial liquid in soup from 6 to 5½ cups. (Oysters add a great deal of liquid to the soup.) In addition, too many oysters add too strong a flavor.

China is for Sundays – *Treat your family as good or better than you do other guests to let them know they are number 1 in your life. Let this be a regular family, sit at the table together, meal with all the good china, crystal and silverware. Don't have any? Use the best you have, it will convey the same love and retain the same feeling of being "special". Maybe the man of the house will take it on himself to cook this meal each week so it is a day of rest for the regular cook. What a great way to show children that "real men cook also". If the children want to invite guests make sure they understand it is a special family meal and be prepared to participate accordingly. Be bold and have guys seat gals at table.*

Shrimp Dip

-----Lip Smackin' Louisiana-----

Let your guests try this before the meal. No need to worry about the conversation, this is a great ice breaker.

MAKES 3 CUPS

1-1½ pounds salad shrimp, or chopped large shrimp, cooked and diced

8 ounces cream cheese, softened

1 cup real mayonnaise, not salad dressing

4 tablespoons bottled French dressing

1 stalk celery, diced or 1 teaspoon celery seed

3 tablespoons green bell pepper, minced

3 tablespoons onion, minced

1 teaspoon minced garlic

juice of ½ lemon

1½ teaspoon, or more, coarse ground or regular black pepper

Tabasco pepper sauce, crab boil seasoning, or Chachere's seasoning, to taste

1 tablespoon granulated white sugar or sugar substitute, optional

Be sure to use cooked shrimp. If they are frozen, defrost and squeeze excess moisture out of them.

Mix all ingredients in a medium size bowl until well blended. Chill thoroughly.

Serve with crackers or chips.

Cocktail Sauce for Seafood

-----Lip Smackin' Louisiana-----

Why purchase commercial brands? Homemade is easy and tastes fresher.

Makes about one cup

½   cup ketchup

3   teaspoons hot prepared horseradish

½   teaspoon lemon juice

     salt to taste

     Tabasco sauce, optional
     cayenne pepper, optional

Mix all together, check seasonings adding more horseradish or a dash of Tabasco sauce or cayenne pepper if you want sauce hotter.

Chill until ready to use.

Bond with extended family and friends with a regularly scheduled meal - *In this era of the nuclear family, only close knit and mostly smaller town families get together very often to have a meal. Dependent upon your family situation, make plans to get together for a rotating home cooked meal at various times during the year. Some families do it every week, some every month while others get together on holidays like Labor Day, Memorial Day and the Fourth of July. Whenever it happens, it provides an interfamily bonding and social interaction that develops support groups and memories forever.*

Tartar Sauce

Nothing tastes better with fish or other seafood than this homemade sauce.

Makes ¾ to 1 cup

½   **cup Hellman's Real Mayonnaise**

1½-2 **teaspoons onion, finely grated**

1½   **tablespoons dill relish**

½   **teaspoon celery seed**

½   **teaspoon lemon juice**

½   **teaspoon salt**

½   **teaspoon ground black pepper**

Mix all ingredients together in a small bowl. Adjust seasonings to taste. Allow to chill for at least ½ hour and stir again before using.

Will keep in refrigerator for several days.

Spicy Butter Dipping Sauce

-----Lip Smackin' Louisiana-----

Big dipper, little dipper, double dipper...this is as tasty as it gets.

Makes 1 cup

1   **cup (2 sticks) unsalted butter**

1   **tablespoon parsley, chopped**

1   **teaspoon minced garlic**

½   **teaspoon cayenne pepper**

1   **teaspoon lemon zest**

      salt to taste

Melt butter in a saucepan and sprinkle in parsley, garlic, cayenne pepper, and lemon zest. Sauté gently for 2-3 minutes. Adjust seasonings and add salt to taste.

Allow to sit for flavors to blend.

Serve warm with steamed blue crabs or boiled shrimp.

A picnic for two - *Blanket on the floor, lights down low, favorite music in the background, chilled wine, champagne or whatever you want for drinks. Use large pillows to ease your seating or stretching out. Some of us are no longer able to sit cross-legged yoga-style, at least comfortably, (and some of us even creak a bit trying to move around on the floor). Just remember comfort is key. You can have scented candles scattered around the room or some incense to set the mood, but if you think your food is sufficiently aromatic, forget the artificial scents. At that point your partner won't care whether you are having hot dogs or filet mignon. This is even better as a spur-of-the-moment evening dinner during lightning flashes, thunderstorms and rain on the roof.*

Sweet and Sassy Dipping Sauce

-----Lip Smackin' Louisiana-----

A quick and easy recipe that can be poured over a dish or used as a dipping sauce for shrimp. This is a sauce that makes good food taste even better!

Makes ⅓ cup sauce

⅓   **cup white vinegar**

4   **tablespoons brown sugar**

1   **teaspoon honey**

⅛   **teaspoon dried cilantro**

½   **teaspoon ketchup**

1   **teaspoon soy sauce**

3   **teaspoons cornstarch mixed with 4 teaspoons pineapple juice**

Mix the vinegar, brown sugar, honey, cilantro, ketchup and soy sauce together and bring to a boil in a small pot.

Add the cornstarch and juice mixture to the other ingredients and stir to thicken.

Serving Suggestions:

If desired, you can add one green pepper, cut into chunks, and pineapple chunks as desired after adding the cornstarch.

For a thicker sauce increase the cornstarch to 4 teaspoons while keeping the liquid constant.

Heavenly Hush Puppies

-----Lip Smackin' Louisiana-----

Hush Puppies make a wonderful appetizer or side dish for fried fish, shrimp, oysters, or other seafood dishes, with or without tartar sauce.

Makes about 2 dozen

1	cup yellow cornmeal
1	cup flour
½	teaspoon baking powder
1	teaspoon sugar
1	teaspoon salt
	dash of Cajun seasoning, or cayenne pepper
1	egg
¾	cup milk or light cream
2-3	teaspoons sweet onion, grated or minced
1	quart or more hot cooking oil

Mix cornmeal, flour, baking powder, sugar, salt and Cajun seasonings (or cayenne pepper) well in a large bowl. Add egg, milk or cream, and onion to dry ingredients and stir until well blended. If adding seafood or corn, do that now and gently mix into batter.

Drop one heaping teaspoon at a time into hot, 350 degree, oil. If you just fried fish, the oil you used works great. Fry until golden brown.

The origin of hush puppies is not clear, possibly being the result of a creative cook choosing to fry rather than bake corn bread. Whatever their roots, hush puppies are served in most all coastal seafood restaurants and can be either plain or with a little shrimp, whole kernel corn, or crawfish tails and a dash of Cajun seasoning stirred into the batter.

Crab or Shrimp Cakes

-----Lip Smackin' Louisiana-----

Try these as appetizers or as a side dish with a seafood meal.

SERVES 6-8

1	cup (2 sticks) cold butter
2	cups onion, diced
1	cup green pepper, diced
½	cup celery, diced
1	teaspoon fresh garlic, finely diced
½	cup crab or shrimp stock, if available
1	cup coarse white bread crumbs (can make with stale Italian bread in processor– do not brown)
¼	cup green onion tops, chopped fine
¼	teaspoon fresh or dried thyme
¼	teaspoon salt
½	teaspoon ground white pepper
¼	teaspoon cayenne pepper
2	eggs, well beaten
	cooked lump crab meat or medium shrimp
½	cup flour or egg white wash (well beaten egg whites)

Melt ½ stick butter in deep frying pan. Add onion, green pepper and celery and sauté well until transparent – approximately 10 minutes.

Add garlic and ½ cup crab or shrimp stock if available. Turn burner to high and boil off all liquid – be careful to stir often. Do not burn.

Turn heat to low and add bread crumbs and one stick butter cut in patties. Mix gently and leave on heat until butter is melted.

Add remaining ingredients, and take off heat. Gently fold in beaten eggs followed by lump crab meat or shrimp. Spread in pan to cool. When cool, using about ½ mixture at a time, form into patties. Either lightly flour patties or dip in egg white wash (well beaten egg whites). Patties may be chilled until ready to cook.

Saute patties in ½ stick butter over medium heat until golden brown (8-10 minutes), turning once. Try not to break patty apart.

Fried Catfish

-----Lip Smackin' Louisiana-----

A staple in Louisiana diets, fried catfish is quick and delicious, served with hush puppies, tartar sauce and cole slaw. For a spicy version, add ½ teaspoon cayenne pepper to seasonings or sprinkle filets with Tabasco Sauce before adding salt and pepper.

SERVES 3-4

6	**large fresh, or frozen and defrosted, catfish filets (or other frying fish)**
2	**cups plain yellow cornmeal**
1	**teaspoon salt**
½	**teaspoon ground black pepper**
2	**cups or more Crisco cooking oil**

Do not dry filets. Filets can be fried whole or cut into 2-inch lengths. Lightly dust catfish with salt and pepper. Put cornmeal, salt and pepper in a brown paper bag or plastic zip lock bag and shake well. Start heating 3 inches oil in deep skillet, heavy pot, or a deep fryer (requires more oil), until hot but not smoking. Oil will be hot enough when you drop a few grains of cornmeal into oil and it sizzles.

*Drop filets in cornmeal bag a couple at a time and shake until coated. Immediately drop the fish into the hot oil, being careful not to crowd fish. Fry just until the fish floats to the surface, turning over if necessary. Drain on brown paper bags or on a wire rack placed over several layers of paper towel on an 11 x 17-inch pan. Repeat process until all fish is cooked.

If recipe is doubled, fried fish can be kept warm in a 200 degree oven until all the fish are fried.

<u>*Thick Crust Crunchy Fried Fish</u>
Pour 1 cup buttermilk in a medium bowl, add seasonings and blend well. Before putting filets in cornmeal (above), dip filets in buttermilk then remove and drain excess. Continue with "Drop filets in cornmeal bag a couple at a time."

Peel and Eat Shrimp Boil

-----Lip Smackin' Louisiana-----

In Cajun Country life is simple, for a one dish meal throw a couple of ears of corn and potatoes in the pot to boil before cooking the shrimp. If you have a hearty appetite, double the recipe. Put it all on a platter and dig in.

SERVES 2

1	**pound large, fresh or defrosted frozen, shrimp***
1	**small onion**
1	**clove of garlic**
½	**teaspoon celery seed**
½	**teaspoon caraway seed**
½	**teaspoon whole spices**
½	**teaspoon ground pepper**
2	**teaspoons salt**
	****or replace seasonings with 1 bag shrimp boil**
	red pepper flakes, a dash or enough to make you sweat, optional

One pound fresh shrimp makes 2 cups cooked and peeled shrimp.

Add all seasonings to a 4-quart or larger pot, filled with water within 2-3 inches of top, over high heat and bring to boil. If you like your shrimp spicy hot, add red pepper flakes to taste. While water is heating, prepare shrimp.

Wash shrimp in cold water, drain well and set aside until ready to use. Add shrimp to pot when seasoned water begins to boil.

Simmer uncovered until shell turns pink, about 10-15 minutes if frozen, about 5 minutes if fresh. Drain and cover with cold water to stop cooking. When cool, drain. Do not overcook - shrimp meat should be opaque.

Recipe can be doubled or tripled.

Dip in cocktail, tartar or Sweet and Sassy Dipping Sauce.

Crusty Pecan Fried Shrimp

-----Lip Smackin' Louisiana-----

Delicious served with tartar sauce, pineapple cilantro relish, honey, or over a salad with a raspberry vinaigrette dressing.

SERVES 4

1–1½	**pounds headless raw extra large shrimp**
2	**cup pecans**
1	**cup plain Progresso or other brand bread crumbs**
¾	**teaspoon salt**
½	**teaspoon ground black pepper**
2	**large egg whites, lightly beaten with 1 tablespoon water**
½	**cup flour**
1	**teaspoon granulated white sugar**
½	**cup cornstarch**
	cooking oil for frying
¼	**teaspoon each lemon pepper and garlic powder**

Peel shrimp leaving the tail on. Use a sharp knife, and cut along the curved outer edge of each peeled shrimp to about ⅛-inch from the other side, being careful not to cut all the way through the body or into the tail. Remove veins or dark lines and carefully press the shrimp open with your fingers to flatten like a book. This gives the shrimp a "butterfly" appearance. Rinse the shrimp under cold running water, pat dry with paper towels and put in a bowl. Work quickly so the shrimp will not get warm. Put the completed shrimp in the refrigerator while you prepare the rest of the ingredients.

In a food processor, pulse the pecans, bread crumbs, ¼ teaspoon each salt and pepper until the nuts are roughly chopped. Transfer the pecan mixture to a bowl.

Whisk eggs with water and ¼ teaspoon salt each and pepper in a container large enough to dip shrimp.

In a cake pan or similar container combine the flour, sugar, and cornstarch and mix in ¼ teaspoon each of salt, lemon pepper and garlic powder. Mix thoroughly.

Cover a wire rack on a cookie sheet with paper towel. Preheat oven to 225 degrees.

Spray, or grease, a 10 x 2.5-inch deep skillet with cooking oil; fill the skillet a little less than halfway full of oil for frying and heat over medium high heat until hot but not smoking. If you have a deep fryer, you can use it according to manufacturer's directions.

While the oil is heating, make an assembly line on the counter next to your skillet beginning with the shrimp, then flour, then eggs, then pecan mixture. Put your cookie sheet with paper toweling on the other side of your skillet.

Dust each shrimp with flour mixture, then dip in egg mixture, and then press into pecan crumb mixture to make sure it adheres. Set aside. (Remaining coating and seasoned flour can be frozen in separate plastic bags for later use.)

Sauté shrimp in hot oil until golden on both sides, about 4 minutes, turning once. Watch carefully. Using tongs, transfer cooked pieces to your paper lined pan. When one batch is done, put cookie sheet in oven to keep cooked shrimp warm.

Seafood Etouffee'

Prefer a spicier dish? Add ground cayenne or red pepper flakes a little at a time until you have the heat you desire. Remember, it will get hotter as it sits. Serve with boiled or steamed rice or Louisiana Dirty Rice.

SERVES 4

1½	**pound peeled and de-veined raw crawfish and/or shrimp tails**
½	**teaspoon each black and cayenne pepper**
½	**tablespoon paprika**
1	**stick (4-ounces) unsalted butter, not oleo**
1	**large onion, chopped fine**
1	**green bell pepper, diced**
3	**cloves garlic, minced**
2	**tablespoons flour**
½	**teaspoon salt**
1½	**cups water**
1	**tablespoon fresh parsley chopped fine, or 1 teaspoon dried parsley**
	Tony Chachere's Cajun Seasoning, optional

In a large bowl, season tails with pepper and paprika and set aside.

In a 3-4-quart heavy pot or a deep frying pan, melt butter then add onion, bell pepper and garlic and sauté well for at least 10 minutes (until transparent), stirring often. Stir in flour and salt, stir until well blended, and continue to sauté for about 3 minutes, stirring constantly.

Add water and parsley (plus optional Chachere's). With heat on medium high, bring liquid up to a gentle bubble, COVER and cook 10-15 minutes to allow seasonings to blend.

Add seasoned tails and any liquid in bowl and stir. When sauce comes back up to a simmer, turn heat to medium low and stir and cook UNCOVERED for 3-5 minutes (just long enough to cook tails). When tails are cooked, no grey will remain and they will be pink and opaque. Do not overcook or they will be tough. Better to undercook slightly as they will continue to cook in the hot liquid.

Shrimp or Crab Creole

-----Lip Smackin' Louisiana-----

You will think you are in Louisiana after the first bite!

SERVES 2-4

1   recipe Creole Sauce below

1½   **pounds raw shrimp, peeled and de-veined or 1 dungeness crab, scrubbed and cleaned**

1   **teaspoon cornstarch dissolved in ¼ cup water**

Creole Sauce

1   **cup chopped onion**

1   **cup chopped green pepper**

1   **teaspoon minced garlic**

2   **(14.5-ounce) cans diced tomatoes**

½   **teaspoon chili powder**

1   **bay leaf**

1   **teaspoon minced fresh, or ¼ teaspoon dried, parsley (or cilantro)**

1½   **teaspoons salt**

½   **teaspoon crushed red pepper flakes, ground cayenne, or Cajun seasoning**

Creole

Prepare Creole Sauce, below.

While sauce is simmering, prepare shrimp or crab. Rinse, peel and de-vein shrimp. If using crab, clean crab thoroughly. Break off claws, remove body shell and clean out lungs, and other insides. Rinse crab under cold water.

When sauce is cooked, add shrimp or crab, bring to a boil then reduce heat to medium and simmer with shrimp for 5 minutes or with crab for 20 minutes, <u>uncovered</u>. Add cornstarch water, stir and simmer for 2 minutes. Adjust seasonings if necessary.

Serve immediately over hot steamed rice.

Creole Sauce

In a 3 or 4-quart heavy saucepan brown onion, green pepper and garlic in oil until tender. Add remaining ingredients. Cover and simmer 45 minutes, stirring frequently and adding liquid if necessary. Remove bay leaf. Use to bake fish filets or to make seafood creole. Serve over steamed rice.

Jambalaya

Jambalaya may be a derivative of the Spanish Paella and is also excellent when made with shrimp.

SERVES 4-6

1	cup chicken broth
1	cup water
6	ounces canned tomato sauce
1	cup onion, diced
½	cup green bell pepper, diced, frozen, or fresh
½	teaspoon celery seed
1	teaspoon ground black pepper
1	tablespoon parsley flakes, dried
3	cloves fresh garlic, smashed, or ½ tablespoon purchased minced garlic
¼	teaspoon turmeric
2	bay leaves
¼	teaspoon or more red pepper flakes for more spicy flavor (optional)
½	teaspoon salt plus more as needed
1	3-4 pound original flavor Rotisserie Chicken
3	links Andouille (Cajun) Sausage or 1 pound other beef/pork sausage
1	package Uncle Ben's Ready Rice, white or brown
	raw chicken, optional

Jiffy Jambalaya

Bring broth and water to boil in a 4-quart dutch oven (or large soup pan with lid) over high heat. Add tomato sauce and seasonings (everything but chicken, sausage and rice), cover and simmer over low heat while you prepare sausage and chicken.

While sauce simmers, microwave rice according to package directions, pull chicken off bones in large pieces and slice sausage into ½-inch thick pieces.

When chicken and sausage are ready, add both to pot, cover and simmer for an additional 15-20 minutes over medium low heat. Taste and adjust salt and pepper as necessary, adding water if needed. Too much liquid will ruin the rice so don't over do it – you can always add more water if needed. Add cooked rice and stir well. Cover and steam over low heat for about 5-7 minutes, but do not stir again.

Let Jambalaya sit for at least 15 minutes for flavors to be absorbed.

Traditional Jambalaya

To make traditional jambalaya, in place of rotisserie chicken, use 8 pieces of chicken or one large raw chicken. Dust with garlic powder and ground black pepper and quickly brown in oil in a large skillet over high heat. Next, brown sausage in the same skillet and proceed as directed. Add chicken and sausage to simmering pot and cook 30 minutes. Use regular white or brown rice (not minute rice) and stir well. Bring to a boil, then reduce to simmer. Cover and steam for 30 minutes, or until rice is tender, but not gummy and most of the liquid has been absorbed. You can always add more hot water if needed to finish cooking rice.

As above, let Jambalaya sit for at least 15 minutes for flavors to be absorbed.

Serve both Jambalayas with green salad and French or Italian bread.

Note: Can be served as an entree with a salad or as a side dish. Jambalaya is also excellent with 2 pounds of large peeled and de-veined shrimp added to recipe or in place of meats. Stir raw shrimp into rice the last 10 minutes of cooking - DO NOT brown shrimp or re-cover pot after adding shrimp.

Chicken with Okra and Tomatoes

-----Lip Smackin' Louisiana-----

I grew up knowing that gumbo was made with a roux base. I have a friend that refers to okra and tomatoes as "gumbo". Whatever you choose to call it, this dish is full flavored and delicious served with or without rice.

SERVES 4

4	chicken quarters, or 8-10 individual pieces
1	cup all-purpose flour, seasoned lightly with salt, optional
½	cup cooking oil
2	medium red potatoes, scrubbed and quartered
1	medium onion, chopped
4	garlic cloves, crushed
1	(14.5-ounce) can diced tomatoes in juice
1	(8-ounce) can tomato sauce
1	(14-ounce) can or 1 ¾ cup chicken broth
½	cup water
1	teaspoon minced dry or fresh parsley
1¼	teaspoons cayenne or red pepper flakes
1	(10-ounce) box frozen small okra, thawed or equivalent fresh

Arrange chicken skin side up in one layer in a large glass baking dish after dusting lightly with seasoned flour.

Heat oil on high in a large skillet until hot but not smoking. Turn heat to medium-high and brown chicken on both sides, 6-8 minutes, being careful not to crowd chicken in pan. When golden, use tongs to transfer quarters to a heavy 7 or 8-quart pot. Lightly brown potatoes on all sides and set on the side in separate bowl.

Pour off all but 3 tablespoons fat from skillet, add chopped onion. Sauté until onion begins to soften. Add garlic and sauté an additional minute. Pour into pot with chicken.

Add diced tomatoes with juice, tomato sauce, broth, water, parsley, and pepper to chicken pot. Chicken will be completely covered with liquid.

Bring ingredients in pot to a boil, uncovered, reduce heat and simmer covered, stirring occasionally to prevent sticking, until chicken is tender, 25 to 30 minutes.

Stir in potatoes and okra and simmer covered until potatoes and okra are tender but not falling apart, about 12-15 minutes. Adjust seasonings.

Louisiana Style Red Beans

-----Lip Smackin' Louisiana-----

Serve these beans over rice or with hot corn bread. Sprinkled chopped raw onion will add another flavor as well.

SERVES 6

1	**pound dried red or kidney beans**
4	**quarts cold water**
2	**teaspoons salt**
6	**slices bacon or 1-2 pounds (Andouille or other) sausage, and/or 1 ham hock (these are seasoning meats)**
1	**medium to large onion, diced**
¼	**cup olive oil, other liquid shortening, or bacon grease**
1-2	**tablespoons fresh garlic, chopped fine**
1	**teaspoon ground pepper, black or cayenne**
1	**quart hot water, more if needed**

Rinse beans well, picking out stones and debris. Bring beans and one gallon cold water to boil in a large pot. Turn heat to medium and boil gently for 5-10 minutes. Stir in 1 teaspoon of salt, turn off heat and allow beans to soak 2–4 hours.

Cut sausage or bacon into 1-inch lengths before cooking. Sauté seasoning meat(s) and onion in a large skillet with ¼ cup hot oil until onions become transparent. Add garlic and continue sautéing on medium heat for about three minutes more.

Bring pot of presoaked beans to boil. Lower heat to medium and cook while seasonings sauté. Add cooked seasonings and bring pot back to a boil, stirring frequently. Turn to medium low, stir in 1 teaspoon salt and pepper and continue to cook at a gentle boil for about one hour, stirring every 10–15 minutes. Do not put a lid on pot. Stir often to release gas in beans and to prevent sticking. Add water as necessary being careful not to make beans soupy – you want the liquid to have a little "thickness" to it.

When beans are fork tender, taste liquid and adjust seasonings.

Original Chicken Nuggets

-----Lip Smackin' Louisiana-----

A deep fryer, instead of a skillet, may be used according to manufacturer's instructions.

SERVES 2-4

1	**pound chicken livers and/ or gizzards**
	dash salt, pepper, garlic to season livers
2½	**cups all-purpose flour**
2	**teaspoons salt**
1½	**teaspoon ground black pepper**
¾	**or more teaspoons garlic powder, not garlic salt**
2	**large egg whites**
¼	**cup water**
	vegetable cooking oil, not olive oil

Rinse livers and/or gizzards and drain on paper towel, then season lightly with salt, pepper and garlic powder.

In a bowl or large zip lock bag, mix flour, 1½ teaspoons salt, 1 teaspoon black pepper, and ½ teaspoon garlic powder.

In a small bowl, use a whisk to beat egg whites with water until whites begin to foam slightly. Beat in remaining salt, black pepper, and garlic powder. Lightly dust chicken on all sides with the seasoned flour and, one by one, dip in egg white mixture. Dredge in seasoned flour until all are well coated.

Spray a deep 2½- 3-inch skillet with cooking oil, add about 1 inch vegetable oil and heat over high heat. Sprinkle a pinch of flour into hot oil. If it sizzles when added, turn heat to medium high. Carefully add pieces, one at a time, to hot oil and fry until golden brown, turning at least once. Gizzards require longer cooking than livers.

Drain on paper towel and serve warm.

Cole Slaw

-----Lip Smackin' Louisiana-----

It is traditional to serve slaw with seafood. For a tasty treat, throw in a few small boiled shrimp or crawfish tails and a dash of Cajun seasonings.

SERVES 8

1	**medium head of cabbage, shredded**
4-5	**carrots, scraped and grated**
1	**cup Hellman's Real Mayonnaise**
2-4	**teaspoons milk or sour cream**
2	**tablespoons finely minced sweet onion, optional**
	salt and pepper to taste
	cajun seasoning

Combine cabbage and carrots in large salad bowl and refrigerate.

In a small bowl, mix together mayonnaise and milk or sour cream, onion (and shrimp or crawfish), and refrigerate for 15-20 minutes for flavors to blend.

Remove both bowls from refrigerator and mix cabbage with dressing. Refrigerate until ready to serve, the colder the slaw the better the taste.

Add salt and pepper, and Cajun seasoning, to taste just before serving. Salt draws juice from cabbage and makes it watery, so it's best to wait to the last minute to season.

Corn Bread Dressing

-----Lip Smackin' Louisiana-----

Making unforgettable corn bread dressing is a multi-step process but worth every minute. First, roast turkey or chicken, then make corn bread, and then dressing. Make it in advance giving time for the flavors to blend.

SERVES 6

Corn Bread

1	cup yellow cornmeal
1	cup all-purpose flour
4	teaspoons baking powder
½	teaspoon salt
¼	cup sugar
1	egg, slightly beaten
1	cup milk
¼	cup cooking oil

Dressing

1	cup celery, diced
2	tablespoons minced garlic
½	green pepper, seeded
½	cup (1 stick) margarine
1	medium yellow onion, from roasted meat, chopped *
	crumbled corn bread from above
2	cups dry Pepperidge Farms herb bread dressing
½	cup fresh parsley, minced or 2 tablespoons dried parsley
	turkey or chicken, diced
3	eggs, hardboiled and chopped, optional
12	ounces oysters, drained, (if you use oysters you cannot keep leftovers safely), optional
2+	cups chicken or turkey broth, as needed* (if you do not have enough 2 or more cups broth from roasted turkey/chicken quarter, add chicken broth to make up the difference)
	salt and pepper to taste

Preparation of Turkey or Chicken

Meat can be prepared day(s) before. For turkey dressing, season and roast ¼ turkey, dark or white meat. For chicken dressing, season and roast ½ fryer or use leftover chicken.

To roast turkey or chicken, preheat oven to 425 degrees. Spray a roasting pan and rack, or a shallow glass baking dish with cooking oil or grease well with oil.

*Take onion to be used in dressing, cut in thick slices, dust with garlic powder, salt and pepper and spray with cooking oil, then lay on rack or in baking dish.

Lightly dust both sides of meat with salt, ground pepper of choice and garlic powder (not garlic salt), and spray with cooking oil. Lay meat on top of onion.

Put baking utensil with meat in oven and roast between 45 minutes to 1 hour depending on size of meat. Check meat after 45 minutes by cutting close to bone to see if there is any pink. If still pink by bone, cook longer. When fully cooked, remove meat and onions to a cutting board and pour juices into a small bowl. Deglaze pan and add this liquid to other juices, then skin, de-bone and chop cooked meat and chop cooked onions*.

Corn Bread Preparation
Preheat oven to 425 degrees. In large bowl, mix all dry ingredients, stir in egg, milk and cooking oil mixing only until blended. Bake in greased 8 or 9-inch pan for 25 minutes until golden brown. Cool and crumble.

Dressing Preparation
Preheat oven to 325 degrees. Saute celery, garlic, and green peppers in margarine until softened. Mix in large bowl with remaining ingredients adding enough broth to make moist dressing. Adjust salt and pepper according to taste.

Bake in a shallow oven proof casserole for approximately 30 to 45 minutes or until center is very hot. Cool. May be stored in refrigerator for several days before baking, or frozen, then defrosted and baked on the day it is to be used. Dressing improves with age.

Note: Double recipe for use with turkey. If you use oysters also, bake on day you are going to use it and *do not* save for later use as oysters do not hold well.

Eggzactly Right Fried Eggplant

-----Lip Smackin' Louisiana-----

These are so good I have seen my husband try to make a complete meal of them.

SERVES 2

2	**large eggs**
¼	**cup milk**
	cooking oil
2	**cups cornmeal (approximate)**
1	**medium eggplants peeled and sliced to ¼" thick slices**
	salt and pepper

Stir eggs in small bowl and add milk. Mix well to form a batter.

Cover bottom of large skillet with ¼-inch cooking oil and heat over burner.

Spread cornmeal onto waxed paper. Dip eggplant slices into batter on both sides and place on cornmeal spread. Lightly salt and pepper slices before turning over for second side cornmeal covering. After covering both sides of eggplant slice with cornmeal, place into hot skillet.

Cook eggplant slices until facedown side is golden brown and turn. When both sides are golden brown, take up from skillet and let drain on a sheet of paper towel.

After draining, put on a plate and serve. Eggplant can be served hot or cold and can be refrigerated covered for 2-3 days.

Southern BBQ Baked Beans

-----Lip Smackin' Louisiana-----

Move over Boston!! BBQ beans go great with grilled meats, potato salad, and/or cole slaw.

SERVES 4

1	**(31-ounce) can pork-n-beans, liquid on top drained off**
½	**small green pepper, chopped**
½	**cup onion, chopped**
¼	**cup firmly packed brown sugar**
¾	**teaspoon prepared yellow mustard**
½	**cup your favorite barbecue sauce**
1	**large link cooked smoked sausage (not Italian or polish), sliced -or-**
½	**pound browned ground beef**
	salt and pepper to taste

Put all ingredients in a casserole dish sprayed with cooking oil spray and stir well.

Bake 35 minutes at 350 degrees, or simmer in a skillet for about 30 minutes.

Recipe may be increased proportionately as many times as you like.

Potato Salad

-----Lip Smackin' Louisiana-----

For variety, try adding a hint of roasted garlic, and/or finely minced white or red onion, and/or bacon bits.

Makes 1½-2 quarts

4   **unpeeled medium size red potatoes**

4   **large or 3 jumbo eggs in the shell**

1   **teaspoon salt**

¼   **cup dill, or sweet, relish, optional**

½   **teaspoon prepared yellow mustard, optional**

½   **cup mayonnaise, Hellman's preferred**

¼   **teaspoon salt**

¼   **teaspoon pepper**

3   **tablespoons finely minced celery or ¼ teaspoon dried celery seed, optional**

Wash potatoes until clean. Put shallow holes on each side of potato. Place potatoes, eggs (gently), and salt in a large pot and cover with water. Bring water to boil. Immediately turn heat low enough to allow water to bubble gently and cover pot with a lid. Cook for 35-45 minutes. After 35 minutes, test a large potato with a fork to see if it feels tender inside. As soon as potatoes are tender, drain water, take eggs out and cover potatoes with ice to stop cooking process. Allow to cool to room temperature.

While potatoes cool, peel and dice eggs, and place in another bowl. Add relish and mustard if preferred. Add mayonnaise (not salad dressing), salt and pepper, and mix well. If you like celery in your potato salad you can add a little finely chopped celery or a small amount of celery seeds at this time. Taste and adjust salt and pepper seasoning if needed.

When potatoes are sufficiently cooled, dice potatoes into a large bowl. Hint: Like potato skins? Leave skin on a couple of potatoes before dicing but too much skin will be overpowering. Add egg mixture to potatoes, mix well and taste again, adjusting seasonings as necessary. Personal taste dictates how much mayonnaise and/or seasonings you may want to use.

I like plain potato salad, so I do not generally get very creative.   However, you may choose to substitute an equal amount of sour cream for a portion of the mayonnaise. Suggestion: Add a small amount of the other flavors into about a cup of the potato salad in a small bowl, mix and taste. If you do not like the new combination it has not ruined the whole batch. Potato salad is best chilled and is always better when it has had time for the flavors to blend, anywhere for a period of a couple hours to over night.

Hints:
Recipe can be increased or decreased at a rate of one potato per one egg, then adjusting seasonings proportionally. This is not an exact science, so tasting and adjusting is an important part of preparation.

For freshness that lasts several days, wait until just before serving to add salt.

Soup day – *Let's take an occasional day to remember how many others in the world live and have a soup day with bread and that is all. It is very good to remind ourselves of world poverty in order to be grateful for all we have.*

Southern Sugahed Sweet Potatoes

This is so scrumptious that I was told this should be in the dessert section!

SERVES 4-6

4	**medium size fresh sweet potatoes, peeled and cut in large chunks**
	cooking oil spray
¼	**cup granulated white sugar**
½	**cup packed, light brown sugar**
¼	**teaspoon salt**
½	**teaspoon ground cinnamon**
½	**stick butter, cut in little chunks**
1	**tablespoon all-purpose flour**
2	**tablespoons water**
½	**cup broken pecans, optional**
¼	**teaspoon lemon zest, optional**
	miniature marshmallows, optional

Place sweet potatoes in a single layer in a 9 x 13-inch glass baking dish sprayed with cooking oil. Pyrex or corning ware dishes are best. Cover potatoes with sugars mixed with salt and cinnamon. Cover with butter chunks.

Using a wire mesh tea strainer, sift flour evenly over potatoes. Sprinkle water over mixture. Bake uncovered, in oven for 1 hour, turning potatoes over at least once during baking. Cook until potatoes are fork tender and sugar and liquid mixture is the consistency of thick syrup or honey.

For a special treat, add ½ cup broken pecans or ¼ teaspoon lemon zest to syrup mixture the last 10-15 minutes of cooking.

Serve warm with roasted pork or roast turkey or chicken. Also good with marshmallows on top and browned under the broiler.

As you can tell from the recipes in this section, the people of Louisiana make an art of cooking and good eating. It is the center of their social activity and much energy and love is put into it.

Humor is also important to engender happy, memory-making meals – relaxed humor that makes you smile often and laugh easily. This is one of the most important ingredients in Louisiana social eating events. People share a meal and they laugh at and with each other. They also play games and everybody from babies to great-grandparents dance.

Humans are the only animals that cook what we eat. In addition to having opposable thumbs, cooking our food sets us apart from other species. We must eat and we enjoy eating; it makes us feel good and ensures our survival if our hunger is satisfied every day. It is also social urge rooted in the depth of our existence.

Food is the tangible reality of security and love

Deep in the Heart of TexMex

Yo te amo mucho

Contents

-----Deep in the Heart of TexMex-----

Big Bend Basin Avocado Spinach Dip

-----Deep in the Heart of TexMex-----

You won't be able to pry them away from this! This is one of those dishes where everybody wants the recipe! A cool, refreshing and tasty appetizer, first course or dip

SERVES 4

1	**cup frozen chopped spinach – defrosted**
1	**recipe Pico de Gallo**
1	**large ripe avocado**
½	**teaspoon lime juice**
½	**cup sour cream (or equal parts sour cream and mayo, or all mayo)**
1	**tablespoon olive oil**
½	**teaspoon finely minced onion, yellow or white**
1	**roasted and mashed garlic clove, or ½ teaspoon finely minced garlic**
¼	**teaspoon salt**
⅛	**teaspoon pepper**
⅛	**teaspoon Tabasco sauce**
2	**cups tortilla chips**
4	**sprigs fresh cilantro or triangles semi-soft Mexican cheese, optional**

Make Pico de Gallo and chill covered.. Defrost spinach on the counter or overnight in the refrigerator.

Peel and pit avocado. Mash with a fork, or cut up with a pastry cutter, in a 2- quart or larger bowl. Blend in lime juice and sour cream.

In a frying pan, add oil and saute onion until soft and clear. While onion cooks, squeeze liquid out of spinach and mince. Add spinach, garlic, salt and pepper to onion and continue to sauté for 2-3 minutes. Set aside. When cool, mix spinach mixture with avocado. Add Tabasco sauce. Stir well. Add additional salt and pepper to taste. Blend in several tablespoons Pico de Gallo. Chill covered until ready to use.

When ready to serve, pile avocado high in middle of plate. Then pile Pico de Gallo on one side, surround with tortilla chips and serve.

For entertaining, Cut 2 tomatoes, or yellow bell peppers in half, each about the size of a baseball. Scoop out and discard the center. Fill with dip and pile Pico de Gallo on top and allow it to tumble down the sides. Dress with a nice sprig of fresh cilantro or a triangle of Mexican cheese and a handful of tortilla chips. Use one for each serving,

Guacamole

-----Deep in the Heart of TexMex-----

Recipe can be doubled repeatedly, amounts are for one avocado per two people.

SERVES 2

1	avocado
1	teaspoon fresh lime or lemon juice
¼	teaspoon salt
1	tablespoons finely minced onion, red or white
2	tablespoons Rotel tomatoes (or diced tomatoes with jalapeno), drained
1	clove garlic, minced

Peel avocado(s), removing dark spots and seed and put in a medium bowl. Add lime/lemon juice and ¼ teaspoon salt. Mash, leaving small lumps. Stir in onion, tomatoes, and garlic. Add additional salt to taste.

Chill thoroughly and serve with crisp tortilla chips. Makes enough dip for 2 servings.

Formal meal surprise of informal foods - *Another party idea can fit whatever dishes or entertaining you want to do. If you have formal china and glassware and you want to show it off, arrange a sit down dinner with it all on display. The kicker is the meal... prepare an extremely informal meal of hamburgers, hot dogs, chile, goulash or whatever isn't considered a formal meal. The reverse can hold true as well. If you want to prepare a special gourmet meal with escargot, foie gras, hummingbird soup, risotto, or other "special" dishes, with an aged wine, then set the table with newspapers, plastic glasses, plastic flatware and paper napkins. This is guaranteed to jump-start conversation... particularly when guests start reading the newspapers at their place setting! If you want to spend some more time...scan newspapers for subjects according to each individual's interests and ensure those articles are at that particular guest's place.*

Salsas

-----Deep in the Heart of TexMex-----

Your tastebuds will beg for more. If you prefer a fiery salsa, add more jalapeno pepper, washed, seeded and chopped. But be careful, these salsas are addictive!

In America, what we commonly refer to as Salsa, the tomato-based spicy sauces of TexMex foods, has now become more favored than ketchup. There are other sauces that fit in the Salsa category that are eaten with chips or used as a sauce in cooking. Our favorites include Easy Hot Tomato Salsa, Fresh Tomato Salsa, Salsa Verde and Spicy Pineapple Cilantro Salsa.

Easy Hot Tomato Salsa

SERVES 4-6

7	**medium roasted plum tomatoes or 2 (14.5-ounce) cans fire roasted tomatoes, drained**
1-2	**jalapeno, roasted, skin and seeds removed**
1½	**teaspoon minced garlic**
2	**teaspoons salt**
½	**tablespoon dried cilantro**
½	**small onion, roasted or raw, chopped small (or minced)**

Roast tomatoes and jalapenos under broiler until the skin begins to brown and char, turn over and repeat on other side

Skin and seed jalapenos. Wash hand thoroughly after handling peppers. Pepper toxins in your eyes may cause serious burns. To begin, only use 1 jalapeno. Discard browned skin from both tomatoes and jalapenos.

Put all in blender or food processor and process until well pureed. Taste to see if it needs more jalapeno or salt. If not spicy enough for you, add the other jalapeno and process more. If Salsa is too watery, put in pot and boil down, stirring constantly until it is thickened. Be careful when heating, if it is already spicy before reducing it, you may find it too spicy when it is thickened. Serve warm with chips.

Fresh Tomato Salsa

-----Deep in the Heart of TexMex-----

Fresh is always best when it comes to tomatoes. The flavor is so good you may want to puree it and use it as a base for TexMex Bloody Mary's. For a cocktail party, add a shot of tequila.

SERVES 4

6-7	**cherry tomatoes or 1 large plum tomato**
2	**tablespoons chopped fresh, or ½ teaspoon dried, cilantro**
1	**fresh small white or red onion, peeled and thinly sliced**
1	**(10-ounce) can original Rotel diced tomatoes and green chiles***
½	**teaspoons minced garlic or ¼ teaspoon powder (not salt)**
¼	**teaspoon salt, or to taste**

Optional:

    fresh lime juice

    additional jalapeno pepper

*Regular petite diced tomatoes plus either one can green chilies or 1 fresh jalapeno pepper, seeded, rinsed, and chopped, may be substituted for Rotel tomatoes

Rinse and dry tomatoes. Rinse and dry fresh cilantro with paper towel to remove excess moisture; then cut and peel onion.

Put all ingredients into blender or food processor except salt and lime juice and pulse until finely minced. Add salt and lime juice to taste.

Makes about 2 cups; serve at room temperature or chilled.

Mi Madre Avocado Appetizer

-----Deep in the Heart of TexMex-----

To make your dip fiery, add jalapeno seeds along with the meat of the jalepeno. This is particularly good served on large tortilla chips with a little pico de gallo on top of each.

SERVES 1-2

1-2	**roasted or raw jalapenos**
¼	**cup fresh cilantro leaves**
1	**large, or 2 small, avocado, peeled, seeded and cut into small hunks**
¼	**teaspoon minced garlic**
½	**teaspoon raw onion, finely minced**
½	**cup drained Rotel tomatoes or diced tomatoes with jalapeno**
½	**cup buttermilk**
	salt to taste

If using a roasted jalapeno, prepare according to recipe Preparing Roasted Jalapenos. If using raw jalapenos, wash and dry jalapeno, remove stem and seeds. Put into 4-cup or larger processor.

Wash and dry cilantro. Put avocado, garlic, cilantro and onion into processor with jalapeno and pulse 1 minute. Add tomatoes and process until smooth with small chunks. Put avocado mixture into bowl, add buttermilk and stir until blended.

Taste and adjust seasonings as necessary. If you prefer your dip slightly thinner in consistency, add a small amount of the drained tomato juice until you have the desired thickness.

Chill and serve with chips or crackers.

Recipe can be doubled repeatedly.

Pico de Gallo

-----Deep in the Heart of TexMex-----

Some jalapenos are very fiery and must be handled cautiously; juice from pepper can cause burns to eyes and mouth. Delicious served as a side to anything TexMex. Salt lightly just before serving.

SERVES 1-2

1-2   **small raw jalapeno peppers**

5-6   **large fresh plum tomatoes, diced**

½   **small onion, diced small**

1   **cup fresh cilantro, finely chopped**

1   **fresh lime**

Carefully remove stem, seed and rinse jalapenos. Finely dice and put in a medium bowl. Wash hands thoroughly when finished

Add tomatoes, onion and cilantro to jalapenos in bowl.

Squeeze juice of lime into all. Mix well.

Chill at least one hour to allow flavors to blend.

Romantic food hints - *Put your valentines cookie cutters to good use all year round. Cut toast into heart shapes, or cookies, or make heart shaped salmon, crab or shrimp cakes. Make your meatloaf in the shape of a heart, or your cake, or buy an inexpensive heart shaped small bowl and use it for dips or puddings or melted butters. The surprise of something heart shaped at the meal quietly says a thousand words of caring. Scatter Hershey's kisses here and there on the table to be eaten after the meal, or sprinkle tiny candy decoration hearts on table. Buy a dish that says "You are special" or a similar sentiment and surprise one person at a time by putting it at their place at the table.*

Pineapple Nut Relish

The lightness and sweetness of this simple relish makes it a delicious addition to fish or shellfish.

SERVES 4

1	**(20-ounce) can chunk or tidbit pineapple**
1	**cup diced mango or other tropical fruit, Optional**
1	**teaspoon white vinegar**
½	**cup fresh cilantro, washed and chopped**
1	**medium to large jalapeno pepper, washed, seeded and diced**
2	**teaspoons cooking oil, not olive oil**
4	**teaspoons lime, or lemon, juice**
½	**cup walnuts or toasted almonds, broken**
½-1	**teaspoon salt – do not add until serving time**

Drain juice from pineapple and reserve juice for another recipe. Toss all ingredients, except salt, in 4-cup or larger bowl until well blended. Add lime juice and nuts and toss again. Allow to chill for 1 or more hours for flavors to blend. When ready to serve, add salt, toss and serve.

Preparing Roasted Jalapenos

Roasting brings out a wonderful heartiness in jalapenos. For roasted jalapeno, careful preparation is important; otherwise use canned, but <u>not</u> pickled, jalapeno. Flavor will be different but okay.

1+   medium to large jalapenos

Do not touch eyes or face with hands while working with jalapeno pepper and try not to inhale jalapeno fumes. Wash hands thoroughly with soap after preparing jalapenos to avoid skin or eye burns, or prepare jalapenos while wearing disposable, rubber gloves.

For one jalapeno, roast oiled jalapeno on a fork over open flame, on grill or broil in oven until skin begins to blister and char. For more than one jalapeno, spray or coat each jalapeno with cooking oil and spread in one layer in an oven proof casserole or on a jelly roll pan. Turn oven or toaster oven to broil and move rack to highest position. Put pan of jalapenos on rack and let broil until the skin blisters and begins to turn black. This can take from 15-20 minutes total. Check often and keep peppers turned so all sides lightly char.

Cool jalapeno, then peel as much as possible; remove and discard stem and seeds. Only use seeds if you want a more spicy dish.

Spicy Pineapple Cilantro Salsa

-----Deep in the Heart of TexMex-----

This fruity salsa is light and sweet and is delicious served as an appetizer with tortilla chips

SERVES 4-6 with chips

1	**(20-ounce) can chunk pineapple**
2-3	**teaspoons white vinegar**
2-3	**teaspoons white granulated sugar**
½	**cup washed and chopped fresh cilantro**
½	**jalapeno pepper, washed, seeded and chopped**
2	**teaspoons cooking oil, not olive oil**
¼	**teaspoon salt**
2-3	**teaspoons lime juice, optional**
3	**ounces pineapple juice, optional**

Put all ingredients in blender or food processor and pulse 10 seconds at a time until well crushed and blended. If you prefer a spicier version add more jalapeno.

Stir well and set aside until ready to serve. Add lime juice and additional salt at this time if you prefer. If you like more liquid, add pineapple juice and stir well. Makes about 3 cups salsa dip.

Salsa Verde

-----Deep in the Heart of TexMex-----

A nice change of pace for those who want a salsa dip but don't like red tomatoes. The flavor will intrigue you.

**Makes approximately
1 pint/16-ounces (recipe may be doubled and redoubled)**

1-2	**roasted green jalapenos**
3	**small or 2 large avocados**
2	**small or 1 large green tomato or tomatillo**
½	**teaspoon lime juice**
1½	**teaspoons minced garlic**
2	**teaspoons salt**
½	**tablespoon dried cilantro**
2	**ounces sour cream**
	tortilla chips

Roast jalapenos, cool, peel, remove seeds and put in blender or processor.

Peel and seed avocados and add to jalapenos.

Wash and chop green tomatoes into chunks and add to processor with lime juice.

Add minced garlic, salt and cilantro and pulse until chunky.

Add sour cream and pulse until almost smooth.

Chill and serve with tortilla chips.

Late night up – *Get kids in bed by 9:00 P.M. or earlier? Try scheduling a night each month, or every three months to let them stay up 'way later to watch a selected movie or play silly family games. Have popcorn and soft drinks. Let them make the popcorn (microwave popcorn is fairly easy), or make popcorn balls or cookies and let the good times roll. At the end of the movie, have a midnight snack and off to bed! Make sure you have cleared the next morning's schedule for late sleeping!*

Buying and Grilling the Perfect Steak

In your quest for a great steak, don't skimp on quality or size - always choose the best grade of meat available and be prepared to pay a higher price. Your taste buds, friends and family will thank you.

- Thickness matters – choose steaks 1-1½ inches thick, the thinner the steak the more chance for it to dry out.

- For maximum flavor and tenderness always choose well marbled meat that has little streaks of fat throughout. The leaner the meat (less fat) the tougher the steak will be.

- Not all meats and butchers are equal – Identify the best in your area. Try a selection of cuts (filet mignon, rib eye, strip, T-bone, or porterhouse) from a variety of butchers.

- Remember that steak labeled Angus, USDA Prime Aged Beef, or other top of the line beef, varies in tenderness and taste of the meat itself from store to store depending on the supplier, i.e. Angus beef at one store may not be as consistently high quality as the Angus beef at another store.

- Beef labeled Choice or Great for Grilling can be marinated for optimum taste and tenderness. There are a variety of marinades available on the market you can test to determine your preference.

- Allow steaks to sit at room temperature before grilling.

- Prior to grilling the steaks, lightly oil the grill rack to keep steaks from sticking (this also seals natural juices).

- Preheat and maintain the grill at 600 to 800 degrees F and keep it at this temperature for 20 minutes prior to grilling.

- Flip steaks only once after searing one side.

- Using tongs or a spatula keeps the natural steak juices from spilling out.

- To test for doneness, do not use a serrated knife. Using the palm of your hand, press on the steak and use the suggestions below to achieve desired doneness.

Note that steak continues to cook after you remove it from the grill. It is suggested you cook your steak less than you want for serving. For instance, if you want medium steak, cook it until medium rare.

Chef's Shortcuts Really Work!

Test steak for doneness by piercing with a meat thermometer. Do this no more than once. If absolutely necessary, cut a very small slit in the thickest part of the steak with a knife. The best thing to do is learn to test doneness as chefs do by using your hand to judge how well the steak is cooked.

- Rare steak will feel spongy like the pad at the base of your thumb and have very little resistance.

- Medium steak will have slightly more resistance and feel firm like the middle of your palm when your hand is fully stretched.

- Well done steak will be firm without give, like the base of your small finger. Steak that comes off the grill well done is drier, less tender and not as flavorful. Recommend you not cook steak to this stage.

This "feeling" method will take some practice and you may cheat by using a meat thermometer for comparison.

Steak Grilled to Perfection

-----Deep in the Heart of TexMex-----

Steaks will continue to cook after taken off the grill, so always undercook a little so it will reach the desired "done-ness" when served.

Angus or Prime steaks of choice

Kosher salt

coarse ground black pepper

garlic powder

spray oil

peanut or other high temperature cooking oil

Steaks should be at room temperature before grilling. Take them out of the refrigerator and the package(s) and put them on a cutting board or pan for seasoning.

Prepare your grill – In order to keep meat from sticking on the grill, oil the grilling surface with a paper towel dipped in a high temperature cooking oil such as peanut oil.

Heat the grill – Preheat grill on the highest heat for at least 15 minutes before starting the steaks. If you have a 2 burner grill, turn one burner on high heat and the other on medium heat.

While the grill is heating, season the steaks, one side at a time, with Kosher salt, coarse ground pepper, and garlic powder (not garlic salt). Spray with oil.

Use long-handled tongs to avoid heat. Use a timer, and a clean serving platter on which to put cooked steaks when they come off the grill. The platter you used for the raw meat may contain bacteria from the blood sitting out while you cook the steak. Don't take a chance, put away the original platter.

Do not use anything pointed or sharp on your steaks or you will lose the juice from the steak. Tongs work best. Rub the ends of the tongs with oil so that steaks don't stick to them when flipping or removing meat.

The hot side (600–800 degrees) of the grill is the searing side. When you can not hold your hand over the searing side for more than 3-4 seconds it is hot enough. You should be able to hold your hand over the cooking side of the grill for 6-7 seconds at most before your hand is too hot. Lay steaks on the searing side of the grill, without touching, and sear for about 45-60 seconds each side to get a good grilled look. If your grill is not hot enough, sear steaks a few seconds longer. There should be dark lines from the grill rack showing on each side of steak. To form a diamond pattern on the steak, shift the steak a quarter turn while searing to create the "restaurant" look. Searing seals the meat and contains the juices. Do not flip steaks more than once before moving to cooler side of grill.

As each steak is seared on its second side, move it to the cooler cooking side of the grill. Set your timer and cook 1-inch steaks on each side a total of 3 minutes for rare, 4 minutes for medium, or 5-6 minutes for medium well done. When steak is cooked to order (rare, medium, or medium well), remove it from grill onto your serving platter. Let it sit for a minimum of 5 minutes (maximum 10 minutes or it will become cold) before cutting or serving. Your steak will be crusty on the outside and juicy on the inside. Letting cooked meat sit for juices to settle applies to all roasted or grilled meats.

Chili de Fuego

-----Deep in the Heart of TexMex-----

When using Habanero peppers, use plastic throwaway gloves and do not breathe fumes or allow them to get into your eyes. After cutting, wash everything thoroughly with soap and water. Add cautiously to recipe to taste.

SERVES 3-4

3	tablespoons cooking oil
2	pounds chili ground beef or stewing beef cubed
1	large onion, chopped
1	tablespoon flour
2	tablespoons chili powder (or 1 each dark/light chili powder)
2	cloves garlic, minced
1½	teaspoons ground cumin
1½	teaspoons salt
2	(8-ounce) Hunt's tomato sauce
1	(10-ounce) canned Rotel tomatoes
2	tablespoons beef granules
1	(15-ounce) can drained kidney, pinto, or ranch style beans, optional
1	fresh jalapeno, seeded and minced or 1 teaspoon cayenne pepper*
	grated cheddar cheese, sour cream, and chips if preferred

Spray a large pot with cooking oil spray and heat to medium high heat. Add oil, beef and onion and fry, stirring frequently, until liquid evaporates and meat begins to brown. Add flour and chili powder. Stir and cook over medium high heat, for up to five minutes to cook flour.

Add remaining ingredients and stir well. Bring to a boil then taste and add more chili powder if necessary. Cover, turn heat to low, and simmer for 20-60 minutes until meat is tender, stirring occasionally. Adjust seasonings if necessary.

Great served with grated cheddar cheese, sour cream, Frito or corn/tortilla chips and/or minced raw onion sprinkled on top.

*Be cautious in using peppers. The chili gets spicier as it cooks and as it sits. If not sufficiently spicy, be sure to add only a small amount at a time, then taste test to see if it needs more.

To add more "caliente (heat)", seed and mince a small Habanero pepper in place of a jalapeno.*

Cowboy Chili

-----Deep in the Heart of TexMex-----

This cowgirl likes to add a can of rinsed and drained kidney beans but I'm told it's not chili when it has beans. Just your everyday warmer - upper when the weather turns cool.

SERVES 3-5

2	tablespoons vegetable oil
2	pounds stewing beef, cubed
1	large onion, chopped
1	green pepper, seeded and chopped
1	clove garlic, minced
1	(12-ounce) can tomato paste
1½	cups water
2	pickled jalapeno peppers, chopped
2	fresh jalapeno peppers, chopped
1½	tablespoons ground chili powder
½	teaspoon crushed red pepper
½	teaspoon salt
1	teaspoon cumin powder

In a large heavy pan, heat oil and brown the beef cubes on all sides.

Once the meat is browned, add onion and green bell pepper and minced garlic. Fry everything for about five minutes.

Add tomato paste, water, jalapeno peppers (with or without seeds), chili powder, crushed red pepper, salt, and cumin.

Bring to a gentle boil over medium-high heat, then turn down heat and simmer chili for 1½ hours or until the meat is tender.

Test for aroma, texture, spice heat and a lingering tingle taste on the back of the tongue. There should be an immediate desire for more to quench the tingle. (If the sauce is too acidic or creates boils on the skin, dilute basic mixture with three bottles of regular beer (not lite) and try again.)

Serve with crackers of choice and a Texas longneck beer or a Mexican import.

Ground Beef Taco Filling

-----Deep in the Heart of TexMex-----

This beef filling can be used for dishes other than tacos. Use some in your enchiladas, soups or even omelettes. Imagination brings flavor and texture to your dishes.

SERVES 5

2	**tablespoons olive oil**
1	**pound ground chuck or sirloin**
1	**cup minced onion**
1	**tablespoon minced garlic**
½	**chopped green bell pepper, optional**
1	**tablespoon ground red chili powder**
1	**tablespoon ground comino (cumin) powder**
1	**teaspoon flour**
1	**tablespoon dried cilantro**
1	**teaspoon salt**
1	**(10-ounce) can Rotel or jalapeno diced tomatoes**
1	**cup water**
¼-½	**teaspoon beef granules (if your ground meat is not flavorful enough)**

Pour oil into a large, deep skillet and bring to sizzling over high heat. Add ground meat. Use a flat edged spatula to break meat in small chunks, turning meat frequently. Continue to cook until there is no longer any pink in meat.

Lower heat to medium high, add onion and sauté about 3-4 minutes, then add garlic (and bell pepper) and sauté an additional minute. Skim excess oil off meat.

Add all remaining ingredients except beef granules, one at a time stirring well after each. Bring up to a boil, turn heat down to low, cover skillet and simmer for about 10 minutes. Remove lid, taste seasonings and reduce liquid by continuing to cook on medium high to high if necessary. Ensure filling doesn't scorch After liquid is reduced to half, skim remaining fat off top. Test seasonings again and add beef granules if necessary. Stir well and simmer a few minutes longer.

Quick Cheese Enchiladas

-----Deep in the Heart of TexMex-----

Enchiladas are another core TexMex dish.

SERVES 3-4

1	**pack chili mix**
½	**small white onion, minced**
1	**(14-ounce) can unseasoned diced tomatoes (or Rotel for spicy)**
1	**(8-ounce) can tomato sauce**
½-1	**cup water**
1	**pack corn tortillas**
5	**cups (40 ounces) or more shredded Three Cheese Mexican Cheese**

Preheat oven to 450 degrees and grease an oblong baking dish with cooking oil spray.

In medium saucepan, combine chili mix, following directions on package, onions (reserving ½ for topping enchiladas), tomatoes and sauce, and enough water to make a thin liquid. Simmer as directed on chili mix.

Quickly dip tortillas, one at a time, into chili sauce, drain and place in baking dish. Spoon 2-3 tablespoons cheese on tortilla, and roll up like a cigar, leaving seam down. Continue until you have filled dish.

After rolling all enchiladas, pour chili sauce on top, and sprinkle with remaining onions and then cheese.

Bake until heated through, chili will barely begin to bubble, and serve immediately with refried beans and Mexican rice.

Super Great Handmade Tamales

-----Deep in the Heart of TexMex-----

Great for everyday meals, not just for holidays. Pop a couple in the microwave for snack time.

SERVES 6-12

5	**pounds boneless meat, single kind or any combination - pork shoulder, beef chuck, round or sirloin tip, turkey breast, venison**
1	**large onion, chopped large**
5-6	**large cloves garlic, sliced**
	salt and ground pepper
2	**quarts spicy bottled or homemade picante sauce**
	salt and pepper (jalapeno, red, white or chipotle) to taste
80	**or more corn shucks**
1	**cup solid shortening or lard**
2½	**cups Masa Harina (corn flour)**
2	**teaspoons chili powder**
1	**teaspoon salt**
1½	**cups chicken broth or water**

In advance - In a large covered pot, simmer meat with seasonings (onion, garlic, salt and pepper) with just enough water to cover, until very tender. Shred meat, removing fat and sinew, stir in enough picante sauce to moisten meat, reserving one cup for later. Make sure it is spicy enough for you. Adjust seasonings adding salt and pepper to taste (jalapeno, red, white or chipotle) and set aside. This can be done as far in advance as you prefer. If you freeze meat filling be sure it is fully defrosted and slightly warm before using.

That day - Gently wash shucks in a water with a little salt to remove debris and soak in clean water for about 15 minutes. Remove from water and gently pat dry.

Mix masa in a large mixing bowl, beat shortening until fluffy. Add masa harina, chili powder, salt, water (or chicken broth) and reserved picante and stock. Beat until light and fluffy or until a spoonful floats on warm water.

Next, spread about 1 tablespoon masa on the top half of one shuck and spread evenly without going all the way to the side.

Put a spoonful of meat in vertical line on top of the masa. Vertically roll shuck loosely with filling, like a cigar, then fold up bottom half. Masa swells when cooked so don't roll up tight.

After all tamales are rolled, lay or stand them in a steamer with several inches of water in bottom. Bring water to a boil, cover and reduce heat to medium low – just sufficient heat to create steam – and steam for two hours. When cooked, very carefully remove from steamer and allow to cool until just warm.

Tamales may be thoroughly cooled and then frozen.

Makes about five dozen (60) nice tamales.

Love at first sight – Romance is in the air – *put a love note sprayed with your most luscious perfume or after shave (guys, girls love this kind of thing) under your honey's pillow inviting said honey to a late night rendezvous in a room you have ready and waiting for honey's arrival. Wear your most attractive p.j.'s or casual outfit and most alluring scent. Turn off the phones. Chill a bottle of wine or favorite drink. Welcome your honey to the table with a hug and maybe a kiss. Have romantic music on low, lights low and finger foods and maybe champagne or wine on a table decorated with flowers, candles, whatever helps the mood. Dance, cuddle, give each other shoulder and or hand or feet massages if you are up to it. Speak softly or just be with each other. Don't give in to suppressed desires. Waiting makes the soul yearn more passionately. Enjoy your date before retiring to a wonderful night's sleep filled with warmth and love.*

Meat Enchiladas

-----Deep in the Heart of TexMex-----

The word enchilada (ehn-chee-LAH-thah) translates to "in chili." One version is simply a tortilla dipped in chili sauce with a variety of filling ingredients placed on the flat tortilla. The tortilla is then rolled cigar fashion and placed in a baking pan or casserole. This version covers the enchilada with a spicy tomato chili sauce, chopped onions and shredded cheese before baking in the oven. Enchiladas are often served with refried pinto beans, Mexican rice, guacamole, pico de gallo and/or sour cream and a basket of warmed tortillas.

Basic Ingredients

12   **corn or flour tortillas (more if making more than 1 kind of enchilada)**

Easy Chili Sauce – makes 2 cups

1   **cup seasoned chicken broth**

1   **(8-ounce) can tomato sauce**

1   **teaspoon grated white onion**

1   **teaspoon red chili powder**

½   **teaspoon salt**

½   **cup water**

½   **teaspoon cornstarch cayenne pepper, optional**

Easy Chili Sauce

To prepare sauce, pour broth, tomato sauce and grated onion in a 2 or 4-quart pot and bring to a boil. Add red chili powder and salt and boil for about 2 minutes while you mix cool water separately with the cornstarch. Add diluted cornstarch to sauce, stir well and simmer 5 minutes. If sauce is too thin, boil it until reduced to a thicker consistency. Be sure to stir often so it doesn't burn. To increase "heat" add a little cayenne pepper. Dip tortillas in sauce to prepare enchiladas or freeze sauce and use at a later date.

Mexican Roasted Chili Sauce
– makes 4 cups

1	pound large round or plum tomatoes
1-2	stemmed jalapeno chilies
1	tablespoon cooking oil (not olive)
½	small onion, thinly sliced
1½	cups chicken broth or
1	teaspoon chicken granules dissolved in 1½ cups warm water
1 -1½ teaspoons salt and pepper	

Fillings for Enchiladas
You can prepare all your ingredients in advance and then assemble and heat thoroughly just prior to serving.

Mexican Roasted Chili Sauce

To prepare sauce, roast washed and dried tomatoes and chilies on a baking sheet under a very hot broiler until black and blistered, about 5-6 minutes per side. Cool. Peel vegetables saving any juice and put tomatoes and juice in a bowl. Remove and discard seeds from the chilies and put them into the bowl with tomatoes. Pour tomatoes and chilies into a blender and process until very smooth.

Heat oil in a medium skillet or saucepan and fry onion over medium heat until browned, 8-10 minutes. Increase heat to high then add tomato-chili mixture. Cook and stir for 5 minutes until the mixture darkens and becomes thick. Reduce heat to medium-low, add broth or chicken granules and let sauce simmer for about 15 minutes until it begins to thicken slightly. Season with salt and pepper to taste. May be frozen for later use or used immediately.

Enchiladas Con Carne

1	**pound ground chuck or sirloin OR**
3-4	**cups leftover boneless roast pork, beef or skinless chicken, diced**
½	**teaspoon each salt and pepper**
1	**pack chili mix**
1	**recipe heated chili sauce of choice**

Preparation of Enchiladas Con Carne

Quick fry ground or diced meat in a hot skillet with ½ teaspoon each salt and pepper until brown. Use spatula to break meat into fine pieces as it fries. When brown, drain well. Add chili mix pack to meat and mix well.

Stir just enough chili sauce into room temperature meat to moisten lightly and then heat just enough to warm filling. Adjust seasonings.

Easy Chicken Filling

4	**large boneless chicken breasts or 2 cups boned and diced cooked chicken or turkey**
1	**large onion, chopped**
2	**tablespoons minced garlic**
1	**tablespoon comino powder**
1	**teaspoon dried cilantro**
2	**(10-ounce) cans diced tomatoes (or 1 (10-ounce) can plain tomatoes plus 1 (10-ounce) can Rotel tomatoes)**
2	**(14-ounce) cans chicken broth, or 28-ounces homemade chicken stock**
½	**teaspoon pepper**
1	**teaspoon salt**
1	**recipe heated chili sauce of choice**

Preparation of Easy Chicken filling

Place above ingredients in 4-quart or larger pot (with lid). If you don't have Rotel tomatoes, add 1 large jalapeno or poblano chile pepper, seeded and minced. Bring to a slow boil and cook for one hour, covered. (Mixture can be made in advance and chilled or frozen and reheated when ready to assemble enchiladas.

Yummy Chicken filling

2   **large frozen chicken breasts (or 3½ cups shredded rotisserie chicken breast)**

1   **(10-ounce) can Rotel tomatoes OR**

1   **(14-ounce) can plain diced tomatoes and 1 (4.5-ounce) can diced green chilies**

1   **(14-ounce) can chicken broth**

1   **cup water**

2   **teaspoons dried cilantro, or 4 teaspoons fresh cilantro, minced**

½   **cup minced raw onion**

1   **tablespoon minced garlic**

½   **teaspoon ground cumin (comino)**

1½   **teaspoons chili powder**

½-¾ **teaspoon salt**

1   **recipe heated chili sauce of choice**

Preparation of Yummy Chicken Filling

In a medium to large saucepan or skillet, combine all ingredients. Simmer raw chicken, until tender, about 1 hour, or precooked chicken until onion is tender, about 15-20 minutes. If using fresh chicken, de-bone, shred and return meat to sauce.

Simple Beef Enchiladas

¼ cup vegetable cooking oil

1+ pounds ground meat

½ green bell pepper seeded and diced

1 small jalapeno pepper rinsed, seeded and minced fine – optional

1 small yellow onion, diced

1 tablespoon minced garlic

1 teaspoon coarse ground black pepper or crushed red pepper flakes

2 teaspoons chili powder

1 teaspoon ground cumin (comino)

1 (14-ounce) can unseasoned diced tomatoes

1 teaspoon salt

water

1 recipe heated chili sauce of choice

Preparation of Simple Beef Enchiladas

Over a medium-high flame, heat oil in a large skillet. When hot, add ground meat, bell pepper, jalapeno pepper, onion, garlic and pepper. Stirring frequently, sauté mixture until brown. Add chili powder, cumin, diced tomatoes, salt, and enough water to make a thin liquid. Simmer 15-20 minutes. Taste and adjust seasonings as necessary.

Drain liquid into another container. It can be mixed with your chili sauce, discarded or used in another recipe.

ASSEMBLING ENCHILADAS

Dip tortillas one at a time, into preferred chili sauce, drain and place in a greased, oblong baking dish. Spoon 2-3 tablespoons preferred filling onto tortilla, and roll like a cigar, leaving seam down. Continue until you have filled dish.

After rolling all enchiladas, pour chili sauce on top, sprinkle with chopped onions and then shredded cheese. Bake in hot oven until cheese is melted and chili sauce barely begins to bubble. Serve immediately.

Fajita Grilled Shrimp

-----Deep in the Heart of TexMex-----

For a side dish, mix pineapple and bell peppers with all ingredients. Alternate chunks on skewers and grill until they begin to char. Place on a serving dish, heat sugar mixture and pour over pineapple and peppers.

SERVES 4-6

¼	cup olive oil
1	tablespoon minced garlic
3	limes

1½-2 pounds large shrimp

1	teaspoon dried or fresh cilantro, finely minced
¼	cup pineapple juice
2	teaspoons light brown sugar
½-1	teaspoon crushed red pepper flakes
½	teaspoon Kosher salt

Side dish

	fresh pineapple chunks
	bell pepper chunks
¼	teaspoon cilantro, chopped
1	tablespoon lime juice
1	tablespoon butter, melted
3	tablespoons brown sugar

Put olive oil and ½ tablespoon garlic in a Pyrex container and warm for about 30 seconds in the microwave. Set aside for flavors to blend. Zest and juice the 3 limes.

Rinse, peel and de-vein shrimp leaving tails on. Put shrimp in a large bowl and add remaining garlic, lime juice and zest, cilantro, pineapple juice, sugar, and red pepper. Toss gently and refrigerate 20 minutes.

Remove shrimp from refrigerator and add seasoned oil and salt. Toss again until well blended. Set out for about 20-30 minutes to come to room temperature.

When grill is medium-hot, thread 4-6 shrimp each on metal skewers and put on a paper lined plate to absorb excess marinade. Put skewers on grill and dust lightly with salt and ground pepper.

Grill shrimp 2-3 minutes on each side until curled and light pink. Do not overcook. Remove shrimp from skewers onto a serving dish. Serve immediately with Spicy Pineapple Cilantro Relish and tortilla chips.

Vintage Mexican Enchiladas

-----Deep in the Heart of TexMex-----

Stacked enchiladas are often found in West Texas, New Mexico and Arizona. They taste the same as rolled enchiladas but are faster to prepare. If your guests want to help, make it a social event and give everybody a task.

SERVES 3-4

2	**tablespoons red chili powder**
2	**tablespoons white flour**
1	**(60-ounce) can tomato juice or soup, or 4 ounces tomato sauce and 4 ounces water**
½	**cup vegetable oil**
12	**corn tortillas**
12	**ounces cheddar cheese, grated**
1	**large onion, diced**
½	**head or 1 bag shredded iceberg lettuce**
3	**large plum tomatoes, diced**

Preheat oven to 200 degrees and put 3-4 dinner plates to warm.

Mix chili powder and flour together in a pot or deep skillet wide enough to lay a tortilla. Add the tomato juice or other liquid and put over a low heat until the liquid has thickened. Remove from heat and put a lid on and let it sit until ready to use.

Put the oil in a 10-inch skillet and when it is hot enough that water makes the grease pop you are ready to assemble. Reheat the tomato sauce until it simmers.

Drop one tortilla into the grease and fry until it begins to crisp or harden (this will be very quick so do not walk away). Take it out and drop it into the tomato sauce. When it is covered with tomato sauce, take it out and put it on a warm dinner plate. You may also put the hot tortilla on a paper towel to absorb grease, then put on plate and spoon sauce over the flat tortilla. Sprinkle with grated cheese and onion or ground meat (leave tortilla flat). When plate has desired number of stacked enchiladas, return plate to oven and repeat with other plates.

I have found that ladies generally will start with 2-3 tortillas and men with 3-4.

To serve, take the plates out of the oven, spoon any remaining tomato sauce on top of each, and cover with more cheese. Finger-feed the lettuce in a circle around the edge of the plates, divide out the tomatoes and put them on top of the lettuce. If there are only two of you eating, just put the leftovers away in refrigerated air-tight containers and use them for a repeat meal.

For variety, you can:

• add 1 pound of seasoned and browned ground beef or pork to the sauce

• top each tortilla stack with a fried egg for authentic Mexican enchiladas

• for more "heat" use Rotel tomatoes in place of tomato juice or sauce.

• if you are in a real hurry, buy canned enchilada sauce in place of preparing your own sauce.

Grocery Day Raid the Fridge Night -*Make grocery shopping day available for a spontaneous raid the refrigerator meal and be sure to pick up some unexpected surprises. Each person can pick out one or two items for the meal and the host (person who called the meal) can pick out three. Don't worry if they use up some of the items you planned to use elsewhere – a quick trip to the store for refills is worth the fun the family will have with a meal of this sort. You may want to have a rotisserie chicken, or frozen pizza, or a variety of sandwich meats on hand – just be sure they aren't such everyday items that they don't spark interest on a raid. Forbidden foods are a great treat for a meal like this.*

Caldo de Res

A soup for all people. Comfort food at its most flavorful. Sure to perk up a droopy spirit. Mexican beef and vegetable soup. You can choose any vegetables you prefer and add more or less of those you don't like.

SERVES 6

1½	pounds short ribs or angus beef chuck roast cut in 2-inch chunks
1	tablespoon salt
1	(14-ounce) can broth, chicken or beef
1	small white onion, cut into 4 wedges
1	teaspoon ground black/red pepper
1	tablespoon minced garlic
2	celery stalks, cut into ½-inch pieces
6	small peeled carrots
1	medium zucchini squash, cut into 2-inch chunks
1	wedge small head green cabbage, cored and cut into quarters
1	medium red potato, peeled and cut into 2-inch chunks
1	green bell pepper, washed, seeded, cut into 8 chunks
1	teaspoon fresh cilantro or ½ teaspoon dried cilantro, minced
2-4	frozen corn on the cob cobbettes
¼	teaspoon ground cumin, optional

Put the meat in a large stockpot, add salt and broth plus enough water for liquid to cover meat by about 6-inches. Add 1 onion wedge, minced, pepper, and garlic and bring to a medium boil. Cover and boil until meat is tender (up to 2 hours). (or you can use a crock pot and let it cook all day while you are gone.)

Add the celery, carrots, squash, remaining onion wedges, and cabbage. Boil for another 15 minutes, then add remaining ingredients and more broth or water as needed   Add corn, bring back to a medium boil and cook for 10 minutes longer.

Ladle the soup into large bowls. Serve immediately.

Terlingua Tortilla Soup

-----Deep in the Heart of TexMex-----

Soup is delicious served with a side of Spanish rice, pico de gallo, or guacamole; put rice in soup after serving and pile pico de gallo on top of tortilla strips.

SERVES 4-6

2½	**(14-ounce) cans chicken stock or broth**
1-2	**(10-ounce) cans Rotel tomatoes, or diced tomatoes with jalapenos**
2	**raw or rotisserie chicken breasts, skin on and cut in bite size pieces**
½-1	**small onion, chopped**
1	**tablespoon minced garlic**
¼	**cup washed and minced cilantro, or ¼ teaspoon dried**
½	**teaspoon ground comino (cumin)**
4-6	**corn tortillas**
2	**cups cooking oil for frying**
1	**small zucchini squash, chopped bite sized**
1	**small yellow squash, chopped bite sized**
4-6	**corn on the cob cobbettes, or 1 cup frozen or drained canned corn**
	salt and pepper to taste
½-1	**pound shredded Three cheese Mexican cheese**

Put chicken stock in a large pot with Rotel tomatoes and chicken, onion, garlic, cilantro, and comino powder. Bring to a low boil over high heat, then turn heat to medium and cook until chicken is slightly tender, 30-45 minutes.

While chicken is cooking, slice tortillas in thin strips and fry in hot oil. Drain on paper towel.

When chicken is tender, add chopped zucchini, yellow squash, corn and salt and pepper to taste. Bring back to a light boil and cook until corn is tender, about 5 minutes after liquid begins to bubble. Remove chicken bones and skin.

When ready to serve, put ¼ cup shredded cheese in bottom of bowl, ladle hot soup over that and top with cup or more of fried tortilla strips. Enjoy!

Spanish Chicken and Rice

-----Deep in the Heart of TexMex-----

A rice cooker works very well for this recipe if you have a very large one.

SERVES 6

1	**whole fryer or 2 cups boned and diced chicken or turkey**
1	**large onion, chopped**
2	**tablespoons minced garlic**
1	**tablespoon comino powder (cumin)**
1	**(14.5-ounce) can plus 6 ounces diced tomatoes (or 10-ounces plain plus 10-ounces Rotel)**
1	**(14-ounce) can chicken broth, or homemade chicken stock**
1	**teaspoon pepper**
1	**teaspoon salt**
2	**cups raw rice**

Place all ingredients except rice in a 4-quart or larger pot (with tight fitting lid). Bring to a slow boil and cook for 30-40 minutes (without lid). Stir well.

Add rice, return to boil, cover and turn heat down to the lowest level. Allow rice to steam. <u>Do not lift lid.</u>

Cook at least 30 minutes or until rice is tender adding a small amount of extra liquid if necessary.

Casa Grande Baked Potato

-----Deep in the Heart of TexMex-----

Nothing fluffy about this recipe. It is a full meal by itself!

SERVES 4

4	**large Idaho or Russet (white) baking potatoes**
1	**(15-ounce) jar or can chili con queso (cheese dip)**
½	**cup Rotel brand diced tomatoes, or diced tomatoes with jalapenos**
1	**recipe Pico de Gallo, or salsa**
1	**recipe Taco Meat Filling**
	salt and ground black pepper
8	**tablespoons butter, softened**
	tortilla chips of choice

Scrub potatoes and dry thoroughly. Poke holes on top and bottom of potatoes with a fork. Bake in microwave on high for approximately 20 minutes, turning over at 10 minutes(depending on size of potato) or in 400 degree oven for one hour.

While potatoes are baking, mix queso and Rotel in a small pot. Warm on the stove over medium heat, stirring frequently. When thoroughly blended and warmed, turn off heat.

Prepare Pico de Gallo, or salsa, and taco meat.

When ready to serve, cut a large pocket in each potato, sprinkle with salt and pepper, and mix 2 tablespoons of butter into each potato. Next heap on taco meat. On top of this add 2+ tablespoons of the warm queso. Crumble chips on top of queso and top with a spoon or two of pico de gallo or salsa.

Serve immediately. Mucho gusto!!

Pinto Beans

-----Deep in the Heart of TexMex-----

One of the core dishes of TexMex food. Known as Borracho beans at TexMex restaurants.

SERVES 8

1½	**pounds dried pinto beans**
1	**gallon cold water**
¾	**pound bacon or 2 links Andouille sausage, cut into 1-inch squares**
¼	**cup cooking oil for frying sausage**
½	**cup fresh garlic, finely chopped**
4	**tablespoons fresh or dried cilantro**
1	**cup white onions, diced**
1	**tablespoon ground cumin (comino powder)**
1	**tablespoon chili powder**
2	**quarts cold water**
1½	**tablespoon salt**
2	**cups Roma tomatoes, diced**
1	**tablespoon fresh garlic, chopped fine**
⅛	**cup fresh cilantro, chopped fine**

Rinse beans very well, picking out stones and debris. Put beans and 1-gallon cold water in large pot and boil gently for 5-10 minutes. Turn off heat and allow beans to soak 2 to 4 hours.

In large skillet, cook bacon or sausage until well done. If using sausage, be sure to add ¼ cup cooking oil to skillet.

Add garlic, cilantro, and onions to hot grease/oil. Sautee until onions are transparent.

Add sautéed mixture, cumin, and chili powder to pot with beans. Add 2 quarts cold water and bring to a boil on high heat, stirring frequently. Turn heat to medium low. Stir in salt. Do not put a lid on pot.

Cook beans approximately 1 hour, until fork tender. Stir often to avoid burning or sticking of beans. Taste liquid and adjust seasonings. Add tomatoes and cilantro.

Warm Big Bend Corn Salad

-----Deep in the Heart of TexMex-----

For more zing, add one minced jalapeno pepper with poblano pepper. If you do not have a poblano pepper, use bell pepper.

SERVES 2-4

1	**large roasted poblano pepper, washed, seeded and chopped ***
3	**tablespoons butter**
1	**tablespoon vegetable oil**
1	**small red or white onion, sliced thin**
1	**garlic clove, sliced thin**
2	**cups frozen whole kernel corn or fresh corn (cut from 4 ears)**
½	**teaspoon red chili powder**
8	**ounces cherry or grape tomatoes, halved**
¼	**cup chopped fresh cilantro or parsley, minced**
1	**teaspoon lime juice**
½-1	**teaspoon salt, to taste**

*You can also use pre-roasted peppers you purchase in a jar at store, drain and dry with paper towel before use.

Warm salad is best if prepared just before serving. You can prepare and set aside until ready to cook.

Coat pepper with oil and put on pan in hot oven, 450 degrees, or on stove burner and roast, turning often, until skin begins to turn black and blister. Put pepper in a brown paper sack or a plastic bag, close and let sit for about 30 minutes. Peel skin from pepper, remove stem and seeds, and chop. Set pepper aside until recipe says to add to corn. This can be done up to one day in advance and refrigerated until ready to use.

In a medium skillet, put butter, oil, and onion. Bring to medium heat and sauté, stirring frequently, until onion is golden. Add garlic and sauté an additional minute. Stir in corn, poblano pepper, and chili powder and cover skillet. Cook until corn is tender, about three minutes. Add tomatoes, and cilantro, and sauté until tomatoes begin to soften, about 2 minutes.

Remove from heat, add lime juice and salt. Serve warm as an accompaniment to meat.

I Love You This Much...

Just Desserts

Contents

-----I Love You This Much - Just Desserts-----

Celebration Coffee Cake

-----*I Love You This Much - Just Desserts*-----

A traditional holiday favorite, treat your family and friends to this delicious cake year after year. Your kids may be as excited to have this cake as they are to get their presents! Umm....well, maybe.....

SERVES 8

½   **cup granulated brown sugar**

1½   **cups pecan pieces, or other favorite nuts, unsalted**

2   **tablespoons softened butter**

½   **stick butter, melted**

1   **tablespoon ground cinnamon**

1   **cup granulated white sugar**

1   **package frozen Parker House rolls (24) or any frozen bread dough**

½   **cup candied fruit of choice, optional**

The night prior to serving, in the bottom of a well greased Bundt pan, sprinkle brown sugar and ½ cup nuts. Dab little butter dots around the bottom of the pan with 2 tablespoons butter.

Melt ½ cup butter in the microwave. Mix cinnamon with white sugar in a small bowl until well blended. Roll pieces of frozen dough, one at a time, in melted butter and then in the sugar/cinnamon mixture. Place in Bundt pan. When one layer is made (about 12 rolls), sprinkle ½ cup nuts and any candied fruit and repeat, alternating spacing of rolls, until all rolls are in pan. Sprinkle remaining nuts over all.

Spray a piece of foil generously with cooking spray and lay over Bundt pan. Put a clean towel over foil and let it sit overnight, away from any drafts. Rolls should double in size.

Serving Day:

Preheat oven to 350 degrees. Remove coverings and bake rolls 30-35 minutes, or until top is golden brown and crusty. When ready, turn pan upside down onto large buttered plate. Let it sit for 5-10 minutes so caramelized topping has a chance to drip onto coffee cake.

Remove cake from pan and serve warm or cold.

Kiss Me Again Carrot Cake

For an anytime treat, try slicing your cake and freezing it in slices or larger pieces to defrost and enjoy another day.

SERVES 8

Cake

2	**cups all-purpose white flour**
2	**teaspoons baking soda**
1	**teaspoon salt**
2	**teaspoons ground cinnamon**
2	**cups chopped or broken pecans**
4	**large eggs**
2	**cups granulated white sugar**
1½	**cups liquid vegetable shortening**
2½	**cups soft cooked and drained carrots**

Icing

6	**ounces room temperature cream cheese**
¾	**stick unsalted butter**
1	**(16-ounce) box white confectioner's sugar**
1	**teaspoon vanilla extract**

Coat two 9-inch round metal cake pans lightly with oil. Flour or line with waxed paper cut to fit bottom of pans and coat sides of pan only.

Preheat oven to 350 degrees. In a medium size bowl, sift together flour, soda, salt, and cinnamon. Stir in one cup of the pecans.

In a large mixing bowl beat eggs on medium with a mixer. Add granulated sugar, shortening, carrots and sifted dry ingredients. Pour cake mixture equally into both pans. Bake pans on center rack of oven for 30-35 minutes or until toothpick inserted near center comes out clean.

When finished, let cool for 5 minutes and invert onto a wire rack. Remove waxed paper at this time. Cool cake to room temperature.

To prepare icing, beat cream cheese, butter, confectioner's sugar and vanilla until well mixed. Blend in remaining cup of pecans.

Put first layer of cake on a cake plate and use ¼ of frosting to ice the top of layer. Put 2nd layer of cake on top of frosted first layer and ice the top of 2nd layer with ⅓ of the remaining frosting. Use remaining frosting to ice the sides of the cake.

Ultimate Chocolate Indulgence Cake

-----I Love You This Much - Just Desserts-----

Since this is my husband's favorite cake, I freeze individual slices and pull them out one at a time as a little surprise.

SERVES 10-15

	flour or cocoa for dusting cake pan
2	**cups all purpose flour – NOT self rising**
2	**cups white granulated sugar**
½	**teaspoon table salt – NOT iodized or sea salt**
3	**sticks solid margarine (¾ -pound)**
1	**cup water**
½	**cup Hershey's Baking Cocoa**
½	**teaspoon ground cinnamon**
2	**whole large fresh eggs**
1	**teaspoon baking soda**
½	**cup fresh buttermilk (or 1 ½ cup milk with 1-tablespoon vinegar added)**
2½	**teaspoons pure vanilla extract**
2	**cups chopped or broken pecans**
⅓	**cup whole milk**
1	**box plus 1 cup powdered sugar**

Spray and lightly flour, an 11 x 17-inch shallow metal baking pan or two 9-inch round cake pans (dry cocoa can also be used) cake pans. Preheat oven to 350 degrees. Mix and sift into a 4-quart mixing bowl, flour, granulated sugar, and salt.

Put 2 sticks margarine, water, ¼ cup cocoa, and ¼ teaspoon ground cinnamon into a 2-quart or larger sauce pan and bring to a gentle boil. As soon as all ingredients are dissolved, pour over flour and sugar mixture and stir until lightly mixed.

In glass measuring cup or small mixing bowl, stir together eggs, slightly beaten, baking soda, ½ cup buttermilk (or substitute), 1 teaspoon vanilla. Add to cooled ingredients in large bowl and mix well.

Pour batter into prepared pan(s). Sprinkle one cup pecans evenly over batter and press slightly into top. Bake for 20 min at 350 degrees or until a toothpick inserted about 1-inch from the edge comes out clean. The finished cake will be fudgy so there could be a little batter on toothpick but it will not look liquid or raw. While cake is baking, prepare the icing.

Icing

In small sauce pan put one stick margarine, remaining cocoa, ⅓ cup whole milk, remaining cinnamon (optional), (peanut butter lovers may want to substitute one level tablespoon of peanut butter for one tablespoon of the margarine – to be added after this mixture is removed from the heat (see below)).

Stir over lowest flame only until mixture begins to liquify - do not let it boil. As soon as ingredients are liquified and thoroughly mixed, remove from heat. At this point add the optional level tablespoon of peanut butter and stir to dissolve. Add one box powdered sugar, 1½ teaspoon vanilla and stir well.

When making a layer cake, divide warm icing and add 1 cup or more of confectioners sugar to one of the halves. Put this fudgy icing on top of the first layer. Top with second layer and then, using remaining warm icing, frost top of cake. Scatter remaining broken pecans over top. If making a sheet cake, pour warm icing over top of sheet cake as soon as it is removed from the oven, then scatter pecans over all.

Serving Suggestions: Ultimate Chocolate Indulgence can be served warm, cooled, chilled, or can be frozen for use later. Flavor peaks after the completed cake sits over night. Ideally, you will impress your guests with a generous serving accompanied by a steaming cup of rich coffee and a scoop of vanilla ice cream. Secretly save the remainder for yourself for those times when you can sit quietly and savor every bite.

Fabulous Fruitcake

-----I Love You This Much - Just Desserts-----

If you don't ordinarily like fruitcake, this will make you a convert. It is so delicious you will crave it throughout the year. In fact, it's addictive! Prepare at least 6 weeks in advance.

Makes 5 – 5½ x 3 x 2½-inch loaves
4-ounces each:

> figs, dried, chunk chopped
>
> dates, halved, pitted
>
> raisins, natural, seedless
>
> raisins, golden seedless
>
> red cherry, candied halves
>
> green cherry, candied halves
>
> pineapple, candied wedges
>
> orange peel, candied

Soak above fruits with ⅓ cup Courvoisier Brandy for at least 2 days in a closed glass container (or use your favorite brandy or whiskey).

½	**pound good pecan halves**
¼	**pound almonds, shelled**
¼	**pound macadamia nuts, shelled**
¼	**pound walnut halves, shelled**
¾-1	**cup all-purpose flour**
1	**teaspoon ground cinnamon**
½	**teaspoon ground cloves**
1	**teaspoon nutmeg**
3	**eggs, large**
¼	**pound butter or margarine**
½	**cup white granulated sugar**
¼	**cup heavy ribbon cane or other molasses with ⅛ teaspoon baking soda**
1	**teaspoon pure Vanilla extract**
	Additional Courvoisier Brandy

Preparation:

Read recipe thoroughly and assemble ingredients before beginning.

Stir nuts into fruits with brandy. With a large strainer over a bowl, drain fruits and nuts well. Be sure to catch all brandy in the bowl below. Allow mixture to remain in strainer over bowl until ready for flour coating. Reserve brandy for later use.

Line loaf pans with aluminum foil and butter the foil well.

Put a shallow pan of water on the bottom oven rack. Make sure it aligns with the middle of the top oven rack. Preheat oven to 275 degrees

In a large bowl, toss drained fruits and all nuts with a little at a time of ¼ cup of the flour until everything is very lightly coated. Spread them out in a large bowl.

If any flour remains from tossing, mix spices into that and other remaining flour.

Using an electric mixer, beat eggs. Add butter and sugar and beat until creamy and well blended. While beating, add molasses with soda and remaining flour with spices, followed by vanilla and brandy from fruits.

Pour liquid mixture over fruit and nut mixture spread over bottom of bowl and mix together. Knead until well blended.

A single recipe makes around 10 cups of batter.

Divide cake batter into prepared pans and pack to remove air bubbles, leaving at least ½ inch below top of pan. If you have batter left, reserve it to make tiny muffin-sized cakes.

Place loaf pans on top rack and bake. Cakes should be ready in about 1 ½ hours. After 45 minutes check to make sure cakes aren't cooking too fast (edges should not get crispy before the top cracks). Hopefully you have a window on your oven and won't have to open the oven door. If cakes appear to be cooking too fast, turn the heat down and put in a fresh pan of cool water. Continue to check frequently.

When there are several little cracks across the top of the cakes, they are done.

Remove cakes from oven and cool thoroughly before removing from pan. After they have cooled, sit each on individual pieces of wax paper or aluminum foil large enough to completely encase them. Liberally sponge brandy over all sides and top of each using cheesecloth saturated with brandy. Wrap airtight in the wax paper or foil and then in newspaper. Put in refrigerator or constantly cool place to age. You can open cakes and reapply brandy every week or two if you want more moisture and stronger flavor. Alcohol will evaporate and leave only the flavor.

Recipe may be increased in total amount as much as you like but must be done by increasing all ingredients in equal proportions. For example, if you double the number of eggs you must double all other ingredients.

Pans for baking Fruitcake

Approximate Pan size	Amount of Batter	Approximate Baking time
8½ x 4½ x 2½-inch loaf	5 cups	2-3 hours
5½ x 3 x 2½-inch loaf	1¾ cups	½ hours
1¾ x 1-inch cupcake pans	1 rounded tablespoon	20 minutes
3 x 1½-inch cupcake pans	⅓ cup	40 minutes

Sugar Glazed Nuts

-----I Love You This Much - Just Desserts-----

Great on salads, sprinkled on desserts or eaten as is.

SERVES 2-4

1	**cup unsalted nuts (pecans, almond pieces or slices, walnuts, cashews)**
¼	**cup white or light brown granulated sugar**
	dash of salt

Put all ingredients in a 10-inch skillet and stir well. Turn heat to medium-high and cook, stirring constantly until sugar dissolves and all nuts are coated.

Pour nuts out onto waxed or parchment paper on a cookie sheet or other flat pan, working quickly to separate individual nuts as much as possible. Cool until room temperature and then break apart any that stick together. Store in an airtight container in the refrigerator for up to several weeks, or freeze until ready to use.

Milk Chocolate Bits and Pieces

-----I Love You This Much - Just Desserts-----

Package candy in transparent holiday gift bags or decorative jars for gift giving. Store in a cool place.

SERVES 10-12

Milk Chocolate

2½   **pounds milk chocolate Ghirardelli Candy Making & Dipping Bar**

Any combination of the following according to preference:

8   **cups nuts, honey roasted almonds, pecans, walnuts, peanuts**

2   **cups each seedless raisins, corn, rice chex cereal and toffee brickle**

Optional:

    dried cranberries or craisins, pretzels, miniature marshmallows, caramel pieces, peanut butter M&M's

The candy making process entails melting chocolate and adding nuts and other ingredients to coat them. Spread mixture on wax paper. Cool until chocolate hardens. Break candy into pieces and package in transparent holiday gift bags or decorative jars for gift giving. Store in a cool place.

Line two to three 11 x 17-inch cookie sheets with wax paper. Set to the side. Make room in your refrigerator or freezer to put pans with candy for a few minutes – pans can be laid on top of other things as long as they remain level.

If your kitchen is a cool area you can also lay cutting boards, towels or pot holders on counter. Top with cookie sheet sized pieces of parchment or waxed paper.

To prepare chocolate, break or cut bar in chunks into a glass microwaveable bowl. Set aside.

Toss remaining ingredients (14-16 cups total) in another large bowl or plastic bag until well mixed. Set aside.

Melt chocolate according to package directions. Be very careful melting chocolate, it can burn if melted too quickly with too high a heat. It is best to melt a minute or two, stirring frequently, and then heat in 30 second increments until it becomes creamy. Once chocolate is melted and free of lumps, add nut mixture and stir until each piece is coated.

Spread candy in a thin layer (about ¼-inch) on the parchment or waxed paper lined cookie sheets and put into refrigerator or freezer to chill. Continue to spread and cool candy mixture on additional pieces of parchment or waxed paper as indicated above.) When cooled thoroughly, break into pieces and put in zip lock bags or candy tins lined with waxed or parchment paper and refrigerate, or keep in a cool location (warmth will re-melt candy).

White Chocolate Nuts and Bolts

See Milk Chocolate Bits and Pieces recipe for detailed preparation using these ingredients.

2.5	pounds White Chocolate Ghirardelli, or similar, Candy Making & Dipping Bar
4	cups corn and rice cereal (I use Kroger Honey Nut Bitz)
3-4	cups pretzels, sticks or broken twists
12	ounce canned mixed nuts or unsalted peanuts
2	cups pecans
2	cups honey roasted almonds

Optional:

1	cup macadamia nuts, quartered
2	cups seedless raisins
	peppermint sticks broken in small pieces
1-2	cups Cheerios®
	toffee pieces

Grandma's Biscotti

-----I Love You This Much - Just Desserts-----

Italian women made these cookies for holidays or special events. They gathered to share the effort as friends and family in much the same way Mexican women share tamale making.

Makes 8-10 dozen depending on size

5	**pounds plain flour**
5	**full tablespoons baking powder**
	touch salt (1 teaspoon max)
10	**eggs**
2	**pounds sugar**
1	**(16-ounce) can solid pound Crisco**
1	**stick butter or margarine**
4-5	**tablespoon vanilla extract**
	milk
	chopped pecans, optional

Preheat oven to 350 degrees. Mix flour, baking powder and salt in very large container. Use whisk to blend instead of sifting.

Beat eggs lightly, adding one at a time. Then add sugar, Crisco, butter and vanilla until well blended. Add this mixture gently to the flour using just enough milk to work up.

Put dough on table and knead gently until well mixed. Cover with towel and let rest 20 minutes

Cut off a small portion (about 2 cups) of dough at a time and shape into fingers or balls (adding pecans if preferred).

-or- Use for cut-out cookies, rolling dough about ¼-inch thick. Decorate with Royal Icing. This makes "bouquet" type cookies.

-or- Fill with fig mixture *to make Grandma's Italian Fig Cookies.*

Bake until barely beige or brown.

Grandma's Italian Fig Cookies

-----I Love You This Much - Just Desserts-----

Bake only one sheet of cookies at a time using the rack in the center of the oven. Fig filling is better if made in advance and stored in refrigerator or freezer.

SERVES 15-20

Fig Filling

3	**strings (or pounds) dry figs**
1	**pound raisins**
1	**pound pecans or peanuts**
	toasted ground orange peel
1	**quart thick fig preserves**

Cookie Dough

5	**pounds all-purpose flour**
5	**full tablespoons baking powder**
	touch salt (1 teaspoon max)
10	**large eggs**
2	**pounds granulated sugar**
1	**(16-ounce) can solid Crisco**
1	**stick (¼ pound) butter or margarine**
4-5	**tablespoon vanilla extract milk**

Fig Filling

Put figs, raisins, nuts, orange peel and preserves through a food grinder or food processor. If figs are dry – then use a small amount of water and work with hands until well mixed.

Cookie Dough

Mix flour, baking powder and salt in very large container. Use whisk to blend and you will not have to sift. Beat eggs lightly in another container, adding one at a time. Add sugar, Crisco, butter and vanilla to the eggs until well blended. Add the egg to the flour using just enough milk to mix together.

Put dough on table and knead gently until well mixed. Cover with towel and let rest 20 minutes.

Cut off a portion (about 2 cups) of dough at a time and roll into a ⅛-inch thick rectangle about 2 to 2½-inch wide and cut into 2-inch wide strips. Lay a small line of filling (like a pencil) down the length of dough, roll up cigar fashion and cut into 1½-inch to 2-inch pieces.

Lay cookies, seam down, on ungreased cookie sheet and bake at 350 degrees until barely beige or brown. Cool on racks. Frost with confectioners sugar icing as soon as cool or store and frost later.

Melt-n-Your Mouth Chocolate Pie

-----I Love You This Much - Just Desserts-----

To measure a dry ingredient like flour or confectioner's sugar, spoon or scoop into your measuring cup and level it off using the back of a knife. Only brown sugar should be packed in measuring cups.

SERVES 8

1	**prepared deep dish pie crust, 9-inch**
1¾	**cups granulated white sugar**
1	**cup all purpose flour**
½	**cup Hershey's cocoa**
¼	**teaspoon ground cinnamon, optional**
3	**eggs**
12	**ounces half and half milk or canned evaporated milk**
2⅓	**cups water**
1	**teaspoon vanilla extract**
1	**recipe meringue or 1 container Cool Whip**

Meringue

3	**reserved egg whites**
½	**cup granulated white sugar**
½	**teaspoon vanilla extract, regular or clear**

Make your own pie crust or use a prepared one and bake until golden brown. Cool while you prepare chocolate filling.

Sift sugar, flour and cocoa (and cinnamon) into a 4-quart saucepan. Separate eggs and put yolks into dry mixture. Reserve egg whites for meringue.

Add approximately ½ cup milk (4-ounces) and mix well. Add remainder of milk and all of the water. Mix well. Cook mixture over medium heat, stirring constantly until it becomes creamy. Filling becomes thicker when cooled. Remove from heat, add vanilla and stir well. Pour into baked pie crust.

Prepare meringue as directed below and place on hot pie, or cool pie thoroughly and top with cool whip before serving.

Meringue

Preheat oven to 450 degrees. Whip egg whites In a clean ceramic or metal bowl until they begin to thicken. Continue to whip while adding ¼-½ cup sugar in a steady stream. Add ½ teaspoon vanilla extract. Whip until whites hold a nice peak when you remove the beater.

Pile meringue on top of hot pie. Put pie on top rack in hot oven and watch carefully, baking only until golden browned. Not all of the meringue needs to be brown.

Place pie on wire rack and allow to cool or until center bottom of pie plate is cool to the touch. Serve or refrigerate.

Bubbles and mistletoe - *On a non-special evening, but one where there is no major agenda to be completed, hang mistletoe around the house, have a small bottle of bubbles available. Put some dance music on and when your partner comes home, invite him into the kitchen. Have your meal almost completed and dance with him/her while it is finishing cooking. Laugh with each other, act silly and bring a sense of fun to the evening. Use the mistletoe (fake mistletoe works also) as often as you want, be childlike and blow bubbles. Serve the meal and keep the conversation light and humorous like it used to be. Have a special dessert of chocolate dipped strawberries hidden in the refrigerator or pieces of his/her favorite chocolate cake or pie that you have frozen and didn't tell him. Let your partner know how much you care and are glad you share your life with him/her. Sometimes we all need to receive that reassurance that the world hasn't gotten between us and our caring has only grown deeper.*

Sweet Tater'umpkin Pie

-----I Love You This Much - Just Desserts-----

This will become a favorite, no matter what the age.

SERVES 12

2	large sweet potatoes

Cream Cheese Crust

1	stick (½ cup) butter, softened (not melted)
3	ounces softened cream cheese (reserve remaining cream cheese for topping)
1	cup flour
1	cup white granulated sugar (or half white/half light brown sugar)
1	cup pecan pieces

Filling

1½-2 cups sweet potatoes	
1	(16-ounce) can pumpkin
2	(14-ounce) cans Eagle brand condensed milk
¾	cup light brown sugar, packed
½	stick (¼ cup) butter, melted
½	teaspoon cinnamon
½	teaspoon salt
4	large or jumbo eggs

Nut Topping

1½	cups coarsely chopped pecans
¾	cup packed light brown sugar
½	cup old fashioned oats
½	teaspoon cinnamon
½	stick (¼ cup) melted butter

Cloud Topping

5	ounces cream cheese, softened
1	cup powdered confectioner's sugar
1	teaspoon vanilla
1	(16-ounce) container Cool Whip
1	cup sweetened angel flaked coconut, optional
	caramel sauce, optional

Move the oven rack to middle position. Preheat oven to 350 degrees. Wash sweet potatoes and poke two holes on either side of potato to keep it from bursting when cooking. Microwave potatoes 20 minutes, turn potatoes over after 10 minutes then finish microwaving. Scoop 1½-2 cups warm potato from skin (discard the rest or enjoy eating while you are cooking).

Cream Cheese Crust

Grease generously a 9 x 13-inch decorative oven proof baking dish or two deep dish 9-inch pie plates. Combine crust ingredients and using your fingers, pat into the bottom(s) of the baking dish(es). Crust will be sticky but it is worth the effort. Bake in 350 degree oven. After crust has baked 5 minutes, remove from oven and set aside. Leave oven on 350 degrees while you prepare the filling.

Filling

Mix all filling ingredients in a large bowl and blend well. Pour filling in crust(s), then return dish to oven and bake for 35-40 minutes for large pan or 25-30 minutes for pie plates. Dish is done when a knife inserted in center of filling comes out clean. While filling is baking, make nut topping.

Nut topping

Blend together ingredients for nut topping. When filling is finished baking, remove pan(s) from oven just long enough to spread nut topping all over top. Move oven rack to next higher level and change oven temperature to 425 degrees. Return baking pan(s) to oven and bake another 5-10 minutes, until topping is brown and crisp. Remove pan(s) from oven and turn oven off.

Cool completely on a wire rack. When filling is thoroughly cooled (several hours), top with Cloud Topping. HINT: When pie is partially cooled but not hot, put wire rack on shelf in refrigerator or freezer and put pie there to speed up cooling. When thoroughly cooled, remove from refrigerator or freezer. While pie is cooling, make Cloud Topping.

Cloud Topping

In a large bowl, mix cream cheese, powdered sugar and vanilla until well blended; stir in Cool Whip. Spread topping on cooled filling. Sprinkle with coconut and drizzle caramel lightly over all. Refrigerate until ready to serve. (Recipe can be cut in half).

Itty Bitty Pecan Tarts

Great snack for when you need just a taste of sweet.

1	(8-ounce) package cream cheese, soft
22/3	sticks margarine, room temperature
22/3	cups flour, all-purpose
1½	cups pecans, chopped
3	eggs, slightly beaten
2	cups light brown sugar
3	tablespoons real butter, melted and cooled
¼	teaspoon salt
¾	teaspoon vanilla extract
4	miniature muffin tins or 2 regular size muffin tins

Put cream cheese and margarine in a medium size bowl to soften at room temperature (at least 1 hour). Cream together until smooth. Blend in flour and roll dough into 48 small balls, each a little larger than a grape.

Place one ball in each cup. For larger tarts, make larger balls and use regular muffin cups. Press pastry against bottom and sides of cups using fingers to line each cup evenly to the top like a pie crust. The finished product is a one-bite pie. For regular muffins line cup half-way up sides. Sprinkle equal amounts pecans in each pie shell. Set aside.

Preheat oven to 350 degrees. Break eggs one at a time into a cup, then put into a medium size bowl. Add brown sugar, melted butter, salt and vanilla and whisk until blended.

Fill pastry lined cups to slightly below top of crust, dividing equally…do not fill to top because filling will expand during cooking.

Bake 15 minutes at 350 degrees. Reduce heat to 250 degrees, bake 10 minutes more. Cool 20 minutes, then place individual tarts onto rack to finish cooling. When cool, store in covered container or freeze in plastic bags for later use.

Banana Nut Dessert Sauce

-----I Love You This Much - Just Desserts-----

This is particularly suitable for an ice cream sundae with vanilla ice cream, or as a topping for cheesecake, bread pudding or crepes.

SERVES 2-4

3	**tablespoons butter**
2	**bananas, cut into 1-inch lengths**
½	**cup light brown sugar**
½	**cup water**
½	**cup pecans or nuts of your choice, chopped**
½	**teaspoon rum flavoring or 1 teaspoon rum, optional**
	bread pudding

Melt butter in a medium size skillet over medium high heat. Add bananas and sauté one minute, turning half way through. Remove bananas and put on the side. Stir sugar into butter in skillet and stir constantly until sugar begins to melt. When melted, stir in remaining ingredients, bring to a boil, and cook on high heat for 3 minutes stirring often. Turn off heat and allow sauce to cool.

Place a serving of the basic dessert in a small individual serving dish and top with a few pieces of banana. Drizzle warm sauce over entire dessert.

Dessert Praline Topping

We're talking about liquid heaven here. As my son-in-law would say, "It's so good I could bathe in it!"

MAKES 3-4 CUPS

4	**tablespoons butter**
½	**cup light brown sugar, packed**
¾	**cup water**
1	**cup chopped pecans, room temperature**
½	**teaspoon rum flavoring, optional**
2	**tablespoons heavy or whipping cream, optional**

Melt butter in a small saucepan over medium heat. When melted, stir remaining ingredients (except cream) into butter and bring to a boil, then cook on a high heat for 3-4 minutes. If using cream, add at this point while stirring briskly.

Serve warm over ice cream or other desserts.

Stress reliever - *Has your partner been working pretty hard? Have lots of stress at the office? On one of the nights when you know he/she won't be working late and will be home at a reasonable hour, set the table with all your good stuff...china, flatware, candles, linen, flowers, a few rose petals on the table, fix his favorite foods, music in the background and you dressed up just for him/her with a favorite perfume/aftershave. Turn the phones off. Prepare the food as early as possible, so you won't have to keep darting in and out of the kitchen. Eat slowly, enjoy the meal and each other, no negative topics of conversation. Just dreams, and gratitude for having each other as you go down life's road. Date night at home, with no particular occasion except the sense of "special" for both of you. Give your honey a head and hand massage – great stress buster.*

Chocolate Ganache

Feeling creative? Try using white chocolate or a combination of chocolates for a delightful change of pace.

When whipped, frosts a three layer cake

8	ounces milk or semi-sweet chocolate, finely chopped, or 1⅓ cups chocolate chips
¾	cup heavy whipping cream
1	teaspoon vanilla, almond or peppermint extract, optional
3	drops cinnamon oil may be added with vanilla for a Mexican chocolate flavor)

Place chocolate in a large mixing bowl, preferably stainless steel or heat resistant glass like Pyrex or Corningware.

Place cream in a small heavy saucepan. Over medium heat, bring to a boil, stirring constantly. Remove pan from heat and pour hot cream over chocolate. Stir until chocolate is melted. Mixture should be smooth. If using extract, add now and stir well. Makes 1 cup.

To use as a glaze, let stand 10 minutes, and then spoon over cooled cake, pastry, or eclairs. To use as frosting or filling, let stand at room temperature for at least four hours, or chill until it thickens and is spreadable.

To whip for frosting, cool ganache a minimum of 30 minutes, 1 hour preferred or until it is room temperature. When it reaches room temperature, whip on high speed for 2-3 minutes or until frosting lightens in color and triples in volume. When whipped, makes enough to frost a three layer cake. Store cake or pastry in refrigerator because of cream base,

Crunchy Microwaved Apple

A new twist on an old favorite that will have apple lovers begging for more. Makes a very attractive presentation and is yummy as well!

SERVES 6

6	**large crispy baking apples, washed, dried and core removed**
1	**cup brown sugar**
	Cooking oil spray
¾	**cup granulated white sugar**
½	**cup all purpose flour**
1	**cup whole oats**
½	**cup room temperature sweet butter, unsalted, not melted**
½	**teaspoon cinnamon or 2 tablespoons red hot candies**
½	**cup walnut pieces (or other nuts as preferred)**
2	**cups miniature marshmallows, optional**
	cool whip, optional

Wash and dry apples. Using a paring knife or apple corer, core apples (remove center and seeds being careful not to go through apple) but making a generous opening in apples for filling. Dry inside of apples and sprinkle lightly with brown sugar. Sit each apple in a microwaveable and oven-safe bowl or cup that has been buttered or sprayed with cooking oil.

Mix sugars, flour, oats, butter and cinnamon in a medium bowl cutting butter in with a pastry cutter or a fork. When well blended, mix in nuts and fill center of each apple to the top with a generous amount of mixture allowing it to spill over into bowl or cup.

Place cups in a circle in microwave and cook uncovered for 10 minutes. (If making one apple at a time, microwave apple for a total of 5 minutes.) Check multiple apples after 5 minutes and cook until they begin to soften.

Remove from microwave and cool 5 minutes. Top with a generous amount of marshmallows. Place cups on a cookie sheet and broil in oven until marshmallows are browned. This will take only a minute or two. Cool at least 15 minutes before serving.

If you do not like marshmallows, delete this step and top with a dollop of cool whip prior to serving.

If you prefer to make one apple at a time, go ahead and make the mixture, use what you need for one apple and freeze the rest in a plastic freezer bag.

Start a family breakfast tradition - *Many families begin or continue traditions by having a special breakfast on Sundays or Saturdays. Dad makes pancakes or waffles (Belgian waffles with different berry sauces are a special treat!) or Mom fixes special blueberry muffins, biscuits and gravy or an egg casserole. Perhaps the older children will cook bacon, sausages or ham to help with the preparation. Whatever constitutes a special breakfast in your culture or family, it is a time for relaxation and bonding after the busy week. Think about using the "good" china each time just to make it more special and get use out of what seldom gets seen.*

Hot Fruit Crisp

-----I Love You This Much - Just Desserts-----

Got a craving for a munchy or something sweet? Keep the ingredients for this on hand in the pantry. It is quick and easy to make and everyone loves the surprise dessert when watching television or playing games - or unexpected guests arrive.

SERVES 6

¾	**cup old fashioned oats (not instant)**
¾	**cup enriched white flour**
¾	**cup light brown sugar, packed**
¼-½	**cup granulated white sugar**
1 ½	**teaspoons baking powder**
½	**teaspoon salt**
½	**teaspoon ground cinnamon - Optional**
1	**stick butter, room temperature**
1 ½	**cup chopped walnuts (or other nuts)**
½	**cup raisins, optional**
1	**can fruit pie filling of choice (Comstock preferred)**

Mix oats, flour, sugars, baking powder, salt and cinnamon well in medium bowl. Cut in softened butter with a pastry cutter. Mix in walnuts.

Preheat oven to 350 degrees.

Spray a 2-quart oven proof dish or a deep dish pie plate with oil and put ½ of the oatmeal mixture in the bottom of the dish. Spread pie filling on top then spread remaining oat mixture on top of fruit filling. Bake for 35-45 minutes or until bubbly and lightly brown.

Serve hot or cold with ice cream or cool whip.

For a fun treat with apple crisp, omit cinnamon and replace with ¼ cup red hot candies.

Recipe may be doubled or tripled.

Phenomenal Pink Fruit

-----I Love You This Much - Just Desserts-----

Extremely simple and quick!! Impressive served in martini glasses with a dollop of whipped cream and/or a chocolate-dipped strawberry, blueberries, or nuts. Sassy in shot glasses with a demitasse spoon.

SERVES 8

1   (24-ounce) container cool whip, softened

1   (14.5-ounce) can crushed pineapple, drained

1   (14-ounce) can condensed milk

1   (14.5-ounce) can cherry, strawberry, or blueberry pie filling

½   teaspoon vanilla or almond extract*

3   ounces softened cream cheese – regular or whipped

1   cup broken pecans, almonds or walnut pieces

* If using almond nuts and cherry pie filling, add the almond flavoring.

Cool Whip should be softened, not frozen. Drain pineapple well and squeeze out excess juice. Combine all ingredients in 4-quart bowl and chill thoroughly prior to serving.

Extremely rich, therefore best served in small portions.

Royal Icing

This can be made to frost Grandma's Italian Fig Cookies.

Frosts 1-2 dozen cookies

3   **egg whites**

½   **teaspoons cream of tartar**

3 ½ **cups powdered sugar, sifted**

In a large bowl, beat egg whites until they begin to foam. Add cream of tartar and beat until the whites are stiff but not dry. Gradually beat in the powdered sugar, beating for about 5 minutes until it reaches spreading consistency. Keep well covered and refrigerated when you are not using. Stir icing before using to eliminate any dry crust on top. Apply with a knife, a pastry cone, or zippered plastic bags.

The icing is easy to tint with food color and hardens as it dries.

Love letters and sonnets are treasures we all love to receive. Write your honey a love note, a sonnet or just a stream of consciousness describing your feelings for him or her. Tuck it in the napkin or under the plate before a special dinner. It will develop the mood for romance and leave an imprint on the heart forever.

For example, I wrote the following note to my husband some years ago and I still feel the same way...

I saw you and my heart leapt...

Who is this man that has captured my heart...

This person who has changed my life,

And opened me to love again?

You are "him whom my heart loves"

And at the sound of your voice,

The feel of your touch, the warmth of your kiss,

My fragile heart faints within me...

Expressions of love as the main course or as dessert can only strengthen family bonds!

Lagniappe

a little something extra...a gift

Lagniappe defines the culinary legacy of always

providing a little something unexpected and extra.

by Robert Sholly

Contents

American Food Morsels

It is hard to identify a specific "American" food. Of course there are the foods that were found in the New World. These included Turkey, corn, beans, sunflowers, potatoes, peppers, squash and pumpkins. These were all taken back by explorers and settlers and are now a part of a world cuisine, much like the foodstuffs brought to the Americas by immigrants.

There are dishes found in regions of the United States that proclaim their local heritage, but they use older styles of cooking combined with local ingredients. After all, there are not that many ways to cook something and I suspect they have mostly been discovered. The microwave seems to be the latest, but there may be other future technical means of cooking food and killing bacteria to make it safe to eat.

When people think of steak, many think of Omaha, Nebraska not Texas or the other cattle states (except those of us living in them). Omaha was the gateway to the east from the cattle raising regions because of its railroad linkages to the eastern markets. Lobsters come from Maine and Alaska, salmon come from the Pacific Northwest, Blue crabs come from Maryland, Cajun food is from Louisiana and TexMex comes from Texas. Of course there are other places where these dishes are found, but those are generally the immediate responses if someone is asked.

Jon Bonne, the MSNBC.com Lifestyle Editor developed a list of 10 Foods that make America great. Accepting the fact that some of them are derivatives of food from other places, they do seem to personify American food around the country. Dishes such as New England Clam Chowder, Pastrami (New York), Shoofly Pie (Amish country, Pennsylvania), Smithfield Hams (Smithfield, VA., Po-boy sandwiches (New Orleans), Fajitas (Texas), Chicago Hot Dogs, Chile Verde (New Mexico) and Sourdough Bread (San Francisco) seem to represent local ingredients, as well as adapting them to new ways of making and presenting them.

After all that is said and done, however, it is academic to try to isolate an American food solely representative of America. As a side note, the statement "As American as apple pie..." is erroneous because apples are originally European and had long been put into crusts. What is American is the technique of presentation…pie a la mode… pie with a scoop of vanilla ice cream on top.

Fusion food seems to be gathering momentum in the culinary department. This takes a food from one place (oriental noodles) and combines it with one from another place (Texas chile) to create a new dish. This is not new. It has been happening since Adam and Eve mixed apples with hummus. It is the way food is transformed into ever expanding new dishes…Cajun and Creole cooking are perfect examples of this movement. Hamburgers are based on a German sandwich, but no one would intimate that the Big Mac was German food.

So…American food? Honey, we have all kinds of American food. Much of it has been grafted, grown, neutered, mixed and blended until it is no longer recognizable as whatever it was originally. However, when we take my 86-year old mother out to eat and ask her what she wants, she invariably says "American food." She means fried or smothered chicken, meat with gravy, vegetables like dried beans and rice, mashed potatoes, gravy, steamed broccoli, sweet potatoes, greens and cornbread. She wants what she has had all her life and that is those foods currently served in small mom and pop cafes, country-style restaurants and diners. If we have to identify specific foods as "American" I suppose her approach is as good as any.

In Down Home Delicious I have brought you some of the recipes that are reminiscent of the foods you ate when you were growing up. I also present you with foods that have been tweaked a bit and, in my opinion, improved upon. But no matter which ones you cook, I think you will find that they are good, tasty and flavorful, no matter what their title.

These are what we cooks along the coastal flavor trail know as American Foods.

Italian American Food Morsels

-----Lagniappe----

The recipes for many of the Italian-style food dishes found in the United States today, were created by Italians after they had immigrated to America. The rich tomato sauces, the creamy Alfredo, vegetable lasagna, macaroni and cheese, and spaghetti with garlic and oil among many others, are dishes not known in Italy before they were created in America.

Unlike Creole and Cajun food, however, which became a cuisine all of its own, Italian American cooking is more one of adaptation of ingredients to a style of cooking, than the creation of a completely different food culture.

Italy in the 1800's was not a country. It was a region of semi-independent city-states and provinces torn with internecine war. Most regions had difficulty raising enough food and hunger was rampant. Finally, in 1871 Italy was united, but the political solution did not solve the hunger problem.

In 1850 only 4,000 Italians were reported to be in the U.S. By 1859 however, thousands began immigrating to the United States. Southern Italians primarily came through New Orleans while northern Italians landed somewhere on the east coast. When Ellis Island was established, they all came through New York. Some reports indicate that upwards of four and a half million Italians immigrated to the United States between 1880 and 1924. No matter where they landed, however, they brought hunger and a willingness to work the hard jobs to earn money for food and family.

In America they could find or grow tomatoes, a vegetable generally only available around Naples. They started gardens and found they could grow whatever they wanted. They could purchase meat and make sausage and mix it all together to form various dishes. They used similar techniques as in Italy, but the foodstuffs were different and more plentiful.

Thus was created the wonderful slow-cooking tomato gravy for spaghetti and meatballs and other dishes. The Italian Americans became the inventors, creators and crafters of marvelous menus. The Sunday dinner became the most important meal of the week and the entire family participated. There were food rituals to be observed and respect for elders. If you were raised in an Italian American family, chances are you ate the Sunday dinner with your grandparents, uncles, aunts and cousins. Business was business, but family was family and any absence was duly noted and commented upon. Food was always a topic of conversation and few recipes were written. How to make certain dishes was learned by watching and helping, with a little guidance from grandma or mama.

The Italian Americans were never far from the land. Even in urban areas, many had their gardens wherever possible. In the south, many Italians became farmers. My grandparents came from Sicily and had a small farm in Independence, Louisiana where they raised a garden, strawberries for market and children. Like most farmers, my grandfather was a hard worker. When he ate, he was served on a platter to keep up the calories and energy and there was always plenty of food. My grandmother made hot breads, suga (tomato gravy), meatballs, spaghetti, pasta, and used corn, eggplant, peas and beans to make other dishes distinctly Italian American. American southern dishes like baked and breaded chicken, roasts, mashed potatoes and gravy also found its way to the table. Like other Louisianans before them, my grandparents combined cooking techniques and skills from the old country with local ingredients to feed their family.

Meatballs and spaghetti, suga, lasagna, artichoke and pasta Alfredo and biscotti are just some of the more popular foods found on the Italian American menu; even though they may not be considered as completely authentic Italian. No matter their origin, they can be found here in *Down Home Delicious*.

Even though Italians did not immigrate to America in large numbers until the 1800's, it is interesting to note that America is named after Americus Vespucci, an early Italian explorer.

Buon Appetito!

Garlic Tidbits

-----Lagniappe----

There is evidence the Egyptians were using garlic for various reasons as early as 3200 B.C. That is over 5,000 years ago!! A more recent record, about 1500 B.C., mentions garlic and comments that garlic can be used for stamina, heart problems and tumors. Tutankhamen, the youngest pharaoh to have held the position, was buried with garlic along with a few gold artifacts. (The records don't mention if the garlic was for maintaining good health in the after life, or to keep werewolves at bay.)

Greeks and Romans also used garlic for a number of things including insect repellent, rabies, leprosy and asthma. The Greek military and Greek athletes are said to have eaten garlic for courage and stamina (first use of vegetable steroids?).

While not banned explicitly, garlic was not used in the early days of the United States. This was probably a carry over from the British tradition of frowning on young ladies who might use garlic, as well as discouraging its use by suitors who might want to court them. However, garlic was finally tossed into the melting pot of the United States by immigrants who traditionally used it in their cooking and culture. But it wasn't until the 1800's that garlic really started being used in ordinary households in the United States.

Not so strangely, the Egyptians got a lot of things right. Louis Pasteur identified that garlic juice kills bacteria as efficiently as penicillin. When medicines were in short supply, the Russian and British military used garlic solutions as an anti-septic and to prevent gangrene in their wounded.

Garlic has now been proven scientifically to have numerous health benefits in spite of its strong aroma (caused by sulfides in its chemical makeup). Some of these benefits are the prevention of arterial clotting, thereby lowering serum cholesterol. The vitamins and sulfuric makeup of garlic fight carcinogens, eliminate toxins, can regulate blood sugar, detoxify the liver and stimulate blood circulation and the nervous system.

The word is that fresh is better than dried, but dried is still good and retains many of the health benefits found in the fresh. For the distinctive odor after eating, some folks recommend chewing fresh parsley or fennel seeds (which have an anise or licorice flavor).

It is interesting to note that licorice was also buried with Tutankhamen, perhaps to go with the garlic.

Garlic has become known as one of the superfoods, so don't shy away from it in your cooking. It will also keep vampires away. We know this to be true because we have been using garlic for years and we have never seen a vampire lurking around our house or our family. Go Garlic!!

Louisiana Food Morsels

-----Lagniappe----

With the exception of possessing the Port of New Orleans, there is nothing to suggest that Louisiana is any more special than other states in the union. However, Louisiana IS unique because it is the only state in the United States to have created its own cuisine.

Louisiana was governed by both France and Spain before being sold to the United States. The Spanish name *Criollo* described those with European lineage and the name Creole was born. Creole food became a blend of French, Spanish and African.

Spain welcomed the French Acadians from Nova Scotia who refused to pay allegiance to the English. They settled in the swamps and backwaters of southern Louisiana and became known as Cajuns. Their food consisted of local ingredients like fish, crawfish, shrimp, local game, rice and local vegetables. Their primary technique of cooking was to throw ingredients into a pot and stew it together. It was not as sophisticated as Creole cooking but the flavors and tastes were just as wonderful. Peppers spiced up the Cajun dishes and the exhilarating zest of Cajun cooking is a trademark today.

Over time, the Creole and Cajun dishes melded together and it is difficult to tell what dish originated from where. The blending of French, Spanish, Cajun and African dishes using local ingredients have resulted in the distinctive Louisiana cuisine.

However, Creole and Cajun jambalayas, gumbo, seafood, crawfish and shrimp boils still constitute the core menus of this amazingly unique state and people. Onions, bell peppers and celery form the Holy Trinity of vegetables in local cooking and most dishes have at least one or more as an ingredient.

People in Louisiana have a love affair with food and it shows wherever you go. A conversation doesn't go very far before something about food is mentioned and they are off and running with explanations of what they had for supper and what they are going to have tomorrow. Written recipes are seldom used, but almost everyone knows how to cook a dish and describe to someone else how to do it. It would be incorrect to say that food is a religion, but there is very little that goes on in Louisiana that is not connected to food or its preparation in some manner. Business deals are clinched over food, entertainment involves food, recreation often deals with food, hunting and fishing are major activities and the results end up in the stewpot or the frying pan and on the table. Food is not just a matter of sustenance for survival; it is an integral part of life and everyone recognizes it as such.

Louisianans consider almost everything as food and because alligator is no longer an endangered species, you can find it on the menus of many restaurants along with shrimp or crawfish prepared in numerous ways.

Foods even in Louisiana are somewhat regional. Southern Louisiana is primarily Creole and Cajun cooking, while Northern Louisiana is more like other parts of the American south with hominy grits, pork, tomatoes, corn, sweet potatoes and beans and peas.

Louisiana is the home of Tabasco Sauce, a very well-known hot sauce that can be found almost everywhere. The US military provides it to its soldiers to spice up their field rations. One must be careful in using it, however. A report from the *Toxicon*, a science journal, says that drinking a quart and a half of Louisiana-style hot sauce will kill you if you weigh less than 140 pounds. I don't think that applies to Cajuns, though.

Cooking, tasting and experimenting with any of these dishes will be a most pleasurable experience. As Justin Wilson, one of a long list of famous Cajun cooks used to say in his wonderful Cajun accent, "I garawntee!"

Bell Pepper Tidbits

-----Lagniappe----

Several hundred years ago, Europe did not have much in the way of refrigeration (except in the winter). As a result, meat spoiled easily and tasted sour after a few days. The spice trade of the Far East brought spices and peppers to Europe to assist in covering the taste of food just the other side of good. Columbus was trying to cash in on this economy by sailing a new route (which he thought might be faster and more direct) to reach India and the Far East when he ran into the Americas. Upon his return he brought back bell peppers along with other types of plants found in the new world. While actually a member of the chile family, Chris didn't know that and because anything that was called "pepper" had market value, he called them "pimientas" which is Spanish for "pepper".

Many people think that colored bell peppers are different species of the same genus. That you can grow yellow, red or orange bell peppers just like you can grow green bell peppers. You can…but not the way you think. These different colors are merely stages of the same plant growth and it depends upon when they are harvested as to which color you have. The color can be green, red, yellow, orange and, more rarely purple, brown and white.

Green peppers are unripe bell peppers, while the others are all ripe, with the color variation. Because they are unripe, green peppers are less sweet and slightly more bitter than yellow, orange, or red peppers, though in cooking they provide a unique and pleasant flavor. The taste of peppers also depends upon soil and weather conditions as well as storage treatment. The sweetest fruit is allowed to ripen fully on the plant while fruit harvested green and then allowed to ripen in storage is less sweet.

Green peppers are a powerhouse of vitamin C and beta carotene…two and three times as much as citrus fruits, while the red peppers have eleven times more beta carotene as the green.

Storing: You can keep unwashed bell peppers in a plastic bag in the refrigerator for about a week. Because they are unripe to begin with, green peppers will keep a little longer than the yellow and red ones.

Roasting and peeling: Cut the pepper in half. Remove seeds AND the white inside portions (the white detracts from flavor). Place the peppers face down on a cookie sheet.

Place the oven shelf in the topmost position and preheat the oven on broil. Broil the pepper halves about 10 minutes or until only the skin is blistered and charred. When ready, put peppers in a paper bag for 15-20 minutes and use a small knife to peel away skin. This can also be done under cold water when in a hurry, but this technique reduces the overall flavor of the pepper.

Onion Tidbits

-----Lagniappe----

The onion… it is one of the most powerful and popular vegetables throughout the world. It has been used as a medicine, a religious symbol a stimulant for physical activity and not least, as a required cooking ingredient either by itself or in another dish.

Part of its popularity is due to its longevity. There are writings of its existence and use for 5000 years or more all over the world. Its exact origin is unknown but some researchers say it was first grown and used in Central or South Asia.

There are well documented instances of the onion in China, India, Persia, Egypt, Israel, Greece and of course Rome.

In India it was used as a diuretic, good for digestion, the heart, the eyes and the joints. Pliny the Elder wrote about how the Romans believed that onions could cure vision difficulties, induce sleep, heal mouth sores, dog bites, toothaches, dysentery and lumbago.

The Roman Emperor Nero ate onions to improve his voice and it has been said that he had just finished a plate of fried onions before fiddling during the burning of Rome.

Early American doctors told their patients to use onions for headaches, snakebites and hair loss.

In actuality, onions seem to have some effect against colds, heart disease, diabetes, and osteoporosis.

While it might be a little anti-social, some research says that if a person eats at least a half raw onion a day, their good HDL cholesterol goes up an average of 30%. Onions do in fact, increase circulation, lower blood pressure and prevent blood clots to a certain degree.

During the Civil War, General Ulysses S. Grant sent an urgent message to the War Department: "I will not move my army without onions." Three train loads of onions were dispatched shortly and the rest is history. Another example of food as a strategic asset in warfare. Of course, Old Sam also may have been intending for the onions to have some effect on the Confederates if the boys got too close to each other.

When working with onions, tearing can be reduced by chilling the onion prior to cutting, slicing under running water and wetting the onions and your hands prior to slicing. Breathing through your mouth also helps while working. Like garlic, if you rub your hands on stainless steel after cutting, it will diminish its unique aroma.

In Nacogdoches, Texas, it's against the law for young women to indulge in raw onions after 6 pm. It is unknown the last time this law was enforced or by whom.

Celery Tidbits

A great number of people in Louisiana are Catholic and have the Holy Trinity in their belief system. In addition to this holy trinity, they also have another holy trinity in which they put much belief for their cooking: bell peppers, celery and onions (in alphabetical order). It is seldom that you will find a Louisiana dish that does not have at least one and very often, all of them as part of its seasonings and preparation.

In addition to its flavor and texture, celery is often grown for its antitoxin effects. In some regions it is perceived as a cleansing tonic after the cold winter months.

Some of the first mention of celery in ancient literature has it originally from the Mediterranean region. There is some evidence that the Romans used celery for cooking but there seems to be a question as to whether the Italians or the French domesticated it as a primary vegetable for eating sometime around the 17th century.

An interesting side note here is that many people associate Louisiana with France and the Acadians tradition. Not so well known is the fact that many Italians settled there as well and brought their home cooking with them to blend with the Cajun and Native American. We have celery used in cooking Louisiana dishes from both traditions.

Celery's primary use seems to have been medicinal and there is some ancient literature that prescribes celery seed for colds, flue, water retention, poor digestion, various types of arthritis and other illnesses.

Celery eaten raw has diuretic properties as well as providing a great in-between snack for dieters. The leaves can be used as a garnish or eaten. If portions of the stalk are liquefied and drunk as a beverage they may be beneficial for joint and urinary tract inflammations, weak conditions or nervous problems.

Celery contains vitamin C and several other active compounds which may help lower cholesterol, be useful in cancer prevention and to lower blood pressure.

Celery truly deserves its membership in the holy trinity of Louisiana cooking.

Tex Mex Food Morsels

-----Lagniappe----

Politics creates and modifies food. The history of TexMex Food can be simple, or complicated.

The complicated version gets into the fact that Texas was settled by Spaniards, French, Mexicans, Indians and folks from the United States. All of these cultures brought something to the dinner table to form a unique cuisine. If one were to be historically precise, much of what is known as "TexMex" is actually because Texans were Mexicans before they were Texan or US citizens. It all revolves around the fact that there have been six flags over Texas in its history, Spain, France, Mexico, Texas, Confederacy and the United States.

The simplified version is that Spaniards came to the new world and blended their food with that of the indigenous citizens. This blend of food came into New Mexico, Arizona and Texas and was further mixed with the local Indian foods. Additional ingredients were added as people from France and the United States came to the region and added their cultural gifts. While the term "TexMex" does not describe well the foods found in states other than Texas, there is still a certain regionality of cuisine. While West Texas TexMex food is different than South and East Texas TexMex food, New Mexico food differs from Texas and Arizona, though when blended with what is generally known as Mexican food, all of it falls under the umbrella of TexMex.

Even more simply put: TexMex food was developed several hundred years ago when Spanish/Mexican/Indian food ingredients were blended with Anglo/European recipes.

As far as the actual name "TexMex" is concerned, the Texas-Mexican Railway was established in 1875. In those days names were shortened in train schedules to save space and the railway became the Tex. Mex. As time went on, the hyphenated form was used in US newspapers to describe people of Mexican descent who were born in Texas, as well as the railroad itself.

It has been noted in several references that in 1972 the food author, Diana Kennedy identified the primary differences between "real" Mexican food and Mexican food found in the US, in her book The Cuisines of Mexico. As far as can be found, the printed term "Tex-Mex" was first used in the Mexico City News in 1973 to describe certain food.

TexMex food has primary ingredients. These are corn, pinto beans, cheese, chiles and onions. It is interesting to note that while there are other ingredients dependent upon the regionality, these are the ones used most. At first, TexMex used beef for its primary meat because of the cattle ranching influence, but today you can find chicken and seafood just as easily on the menu. Of course there are always frijoles (ordinarily pinto beans) cooked, mashed and fried (refried is a misnomer since they generally have not been fried the first time) and spices only contained by the imagination of the cook.

Like Chop Suey, which may be a San Francisco invention by Chinese-Americans (in recent years there seems to be a question about that), there are many TexMex dishes that have no base anywhere else except from the TexMex food movement. Some of these are nachos, crispy tacos, crispy chalupas, chili con queso, chili con carne, chili gravy and fajitas (fa-hee-tas). Chili con queso (primarily melted cheddar cheese with chili in it) was originated in the early 20th century when yellow cheese became popular in the southwest from the dairy states. There is a school of thought that chili con carne (cooked ground beef with chili and spices) was invented when Canary Islanders came to the US and integrated their recipes with those already here. Fajitas are primarily strips of beef, sometimes marinated and then grilled, to be rolled or folded into a corn or flour tortilla with other ingredients such as grilled onion, chili, bits of tomato, grilled bell pepper, chopped raw onion and avocado.

The *tortilla* is a primary focal point in a dish and the name of the dish is dependent upon how it is formed or used. For example: *Enchiladas* in West Texas and New Mexico are often stacked with flat *tortillas*, while elsewhere the *tortillas* are rolled. However, the ingredients are the same. A *Taco* is a *tortilla* folded in half and fried to form a pocket, with the same ingredients as an *enchilada*. A *Burrito* is a soft rolled *tortilla* with similar ingredients. A *Tostada* is a flat fried *tortilla* covered with bean paste and additional ingredients such as onion, cheese, ground meat, lettuce, tomatoes. *Chalupas* and *Quesadillas* also use the *tortilla* as the primary holder of fillings and have different forms, but often similar ingredients. Many new recipes for TexMex food are extreme variations of the old forms using new ingredients…many have never seen the southwest or Mexico, but still have their fan clubs. TexMex has become a style of food that is still expanding and evolving…however, some of the older recipes are still the best.

Habanero chili peppers are now moving into vogue and challenging the *jalapeño* for room in the *salsa*. It is said that in 1994 a Red Savina *Habanero* tested in at 577,000 units, making it the hottest pepper on record.

The best relief for a burning mouth is milk, yogurt or sour cream. (You will note that many restaurants serve sour cream with their dishes. They may not know why, but there you have it). These foods contain a protein that reduces the interaction pepper has with the mouth's pain sensors…

As an interesting side note on TexMex popularity, *Salsa* now outranks ketchup as the number one condiment in the US.

Tamale Tidbits

-----Lagniappe----

A tamale is an interesting Latino and TexMex phenomenon. It may have even been one of the first fast foods or Meals Ready to Eat (MREs) of the world.

Many of the South and Central American cultures were warlike and needed trail and battle food (hence the reference to MREs) and it was time consuming for women to travel with armies or war parties and cook food for the men. It is now speculated that some women figured if they could develop a food that could be carried by the warriors, not so many women would be required on the trail and could stay at home, eat chocolate (a favored and sacred bit of Mexican food) and create more recipes. Thus the *tamale* was created. Women figured how to cook travel food which could be made ahead and wrapped for travel. Tamales could be heated or eaten cold and could be kept in baskets or pouches. This enabled men to travel faster and to have stamina and energy as necessary for travel or battle. This could be an instance of where a food provided a tactical advantage. However, once a weapon is known, it is duplicated or countered as the creating culture lost its monopoly, the tamale soon spread throughout the New World.

Tamales consist of a dough made of corn flour (*masa*), flattened into small patties with a meat filling or other foodstuff placed in the middle of the patty. It is then rolled to resemble a doughy hot dog, which places the filling in the middle and wrapped with a soft material to hold it together. These were put in baskets and steamed, placed on grills over an open fire or allowed to bake in an oven.

When first created, the wrappings were whatever was available. Banana and avocado leaves and cornhusks were the most common, but fabric, or even soft tree bark made excellent food holding materials; anything which could be folded to create an envelope and keep the food from falling out or being contaminated.

The making of the corn flour (nowadays purchased) and the preparation of the basic corn flour patty, took a great deal of effort and time. Even with the advent of packaged corn flour (*masa*), making tamales still takes some time since each one is rolled by hand, but the effort is worth the effort!! Women in a family often banded together to make dozens of tamales at a time; thereby creating a tradition that is still followed in many places. The tamale party is a fun event that provides a special bonding and develops a closeness that is all too rare in today's high speed cultures. Even if you make tamales by yourself in the privacy of your own kitchen, you are following a tradition that has been in existence for thousands of years and in the process are cooking one of the tastiest meal/snacks ever created.

The above explanation describes the basics of how the tamale is prepared, but there are numerous recipes for making the corn dough, from adding water, chicken broth or other liquid to make the dough workable. The fillings range from pork, beef, chicken, cheese and even various kinds of dried fruits. Over hundreds of years the most common types have become chicken, pork, beef, red and green chili, cheese, and more lately, vegetarian tamales with only vegetables as filling.

Tacos today and Tamale the world!!!

How Long Will it Keep?

-----Lagniappe----

Food	Freezer	Refrigerator
Raw chicken or turkey	6-12 months	1-2 days
Raw beef roasts or steaks	6-12 months	3-5 days
Raw lamb roasts or chop	6-9 months	3-5 days
Cooked leftover chicken or turkey	4-6 months	3-4 days
Cooked leftover meat	2-3 months	3-4 days
Cooked leftover fish	3 months	3-4 days
*Cooked leftover stuffing *Stuffing that was cooked separately	1 month	3-4 days

Source: FDA Publication No. 03-1300

Talking Temperatures

-----Lagniappe----

Food	Freezer
Beef, veal, or lamb roasts, steaks or chops	160 degrees
Ground Chicken or Turkey	165 degrees
Ground beef, veal, lamb or pork	180 degrees
Leftovers and casseroles	165 degrees
Pork Roasts, steaks, or chops	160-170 degrees
Stuffing, alone or in the bird	165 degrees
Whole chicken or turkey	180 degrees

Source: FDA Publication No. 03-1300

Recommended Pantry List

-----Lagniappe----

- ☐ balsamic vinegar
- ☐ bay leaves
- ☐ bread
- ☐ brown and white sugar
- ☐ butter
- ☐ canned tomatoes
- ☐ chicken stock
- ☐ chocolate
- ☐ coffee
- ☐ crushed red pepper
- ☐ dairy products (cheese to butter)
- ☐ Dijon Mustard
- ☐ dry pasta
- ☐ cayenne
- ☐ chili powder
- ☐ cilantro
- ☐ dried beans
- ☐ dried parsley
- ☐ flour
- ☐ flour, all purpose
- ☐ fresh ground pepper
- ☐ garlic
- ☐ garlic salt
- ☐ garlic powder
- ☐ gelatin
- ☐ jelly
- ☐ kosher salt
- ☐ olive oil, extra virgin
- ☐ olives
- ☐ onion
- ☐ parsley
- ☐ peanut butter

- ☐ potatoes
- ☐ red pepper flakes
- ☐ red wine vinegar
- ☐ salt
- ☐ vanilla
- ☐ vegetable oil
- ☐ white pepper

Refrigerated

- ☐ cheese - mozzarella, balls, fresh
- ☐ eggs
- ☐ fish
- ☐ fresh cilantro
- ☐ fresh herbs
- ☐ fresh lemon juice
- ☐ heavy cream
- ☐ lemon juice
- ☐ margarine
- ☐ mayonnaise
- ☐ meat
- ☐ milk
- ☐ mushrooms
- ☐ spicy sausage

Canned Goods

- ☐ artichoke hearts or bottoms, 14 oz can canned
- ☐ broth- beef, canned (14/32 oz)
- ☐ broth- chicken, canned
- ☐ broth- turkey, canned
- ☐ chicken- canned, premium chunk white in water
- ☐ chili con queso (cheese dip) - jar or can
- ☐ chilies - green, canned, diced
- ☐ corn - canned, fiesta
- ☐ corn-creamstyle, canned
- ☐ milk- condensed, Eagle Brand
- ☐ olives - stuffed green or pitted black
- ☐ olives- black, sliced and chopped
- ☐ orange segments - canned mandarin
- ☐ peas-green, sweet petite, canned
- ☐ pie filling - canned, cherry or strawberry
- ☐ pineapple - crushed, canned
- ☐ pork-n-beans - canned, Campbells
- ☐ pumpkin - canned
- ☐ tomato paste-Contadina is best
- ☐ rotel canned tomatoes
- ☐ chicken broth, canned
- ☐ tomato paste
- ☐ tomatoes
- ☐ tomato sauce-small can

- ☐ tomatoes- diced tomatoes with jalapenos, Rotel brand
- ☐ tomatoes- petite diced with liquid
- ☐ tomatoes- small can, diced
- ☐ tomatoes-crushed , canned
- ☐ tomatoes-diced, canned
- ☐ water chestnuts

Additional Pantry Items

- ☐ barbecue sauce
- ☐ beans - dry, pinto
- ☐ beans - dry, red or kidney
- ☐ beans - dry, white or navy
- ☐ caramel - pieces
- ☐ caramel - sauce
- ☐ cheese - parmesan, grated
- ☐ cherries - maraschino
- ☐ chocolate - milk or semi-sweet pieces
- ☐ chocolate - milk, Ghirardelli Candy Making & Dipping Bar
- ☐ chocolate - syrup
- ☐ Chocolate - White Chocolate Ghirardelli, or similar, Candy Making & Dipping Bar
- ☐ cocoa powder
- ☐ coconut - angel hair, sweetened
- ☐ cooking oil - peanut or other high temperature

- ☐ cooking oil - spray
- ☐ cooking oil - vegetable
- ☐ corn shucks
- ☐ crackers- club or saltine
- ☐ croutons
- ☐ dates- pitted
- ☐ dressing- French, bottled
- ☐ juice
- ☐ M&M's- peanut butter
- ☐ figs- dried
- ☐ herb bread dressing
- ☐ marshmallow- crème, jar
- ☐ marshmallows - miniature
- ☐ molasses - heavy ribbon cane or other
- ☐ mushrooms
- ☐ mustard - Dijon
- ☐ mustard- yellow
- ☐ mustard - yellow, prepared
- ☐ noodles - fettuccini
- ☐ nuts - almonds, whole or sliced
- ☐ nuts - pecans
- ☐ nuts - walnuts
- ☐ nuts- macadamia
- ☐ nuts - almonds, honey roasted
- ☐ nuts - pistachio, roasted
- ☐ oil- olive, extra-virgin
- ☐ oil - olive, classic or light
- ☐ orange peel - toasted, ground
- ☐ pasta - lasagna noodles

- ☐ pasta - macaroni, dry small shell or elbow
- ☐ pasta - macaroni, small bowtie Pepperidge Farms, dry
- ☐ pasta - small
- ☐ pasta - spaghetti, vermicelli
- ☐ honey
- ☐ horseradish - hot, prepared
- ☐ ketchup
- ☐ lemon
- ☐ pickle relish - dill (or sweet)
- ☐ pineapple - juice
- ☐ pretzels
- ☐ raisins - golden, seedless
- ☐ raisins - natural, seedless
- ☐ rice - brown
- ☐ rice - long grain white rice (not parboiled)
- ☐ rice- raw
- ☐ shortening - solid or lard
- ☐ toffee- pieces
- ☐ tortillas - corn
- ☐ Vinegar - balsamic or other vinegar of choice
- ☐ vinegar - red wine
- ☐ wine - red

Some Basic Substitutions

Alcohol Products

Brandy or rum, 2 tablespoons
1 /2 to 1 teaspoon brandy or rum extract

Red wine, 1 /4 cup or more
Equal measure of red grape juice or cranberry juice

White wine, 1 /4 cup or more
Equal measure of white grape juice or apple juice.
Add water, white grape juice, or apple juice to get the specified
amount of liquid (when the liquid amount is crucial)

Baking Products

Semisweet Chocolate, 1 ounce
1 ounce unsweetened chocolate plus 1 tablespoon sugar

Unsweetened Chocolate, 1 ounce or square
3 tablespoons cocoa plus 1 tablespoon fat, or 1 ounce semisweet chips
-or- 1 ounce square semisweet chocolate chips, semisweet, 6-ounce package, melted
-or- 2 ounces unsweetened chocolate, 2 tablespoons shortening plus 1 /2 cup sugar

Cocoa, 1 /4 cup
1 ounce unsweetened chocolate (decrease fat in recipe by 1 1/2 teaspoons)

Cornstarch, 1 tablespoon
2 tablespoons all-purpose flour

Corn syrup, light, 1 /2 cup
1 /2 cup sugar plus 2 tablespoons water

-----Lagniappe----

<u>All-purpose flour, 1 cup sifted</u>
1 cup plus 2 tablespoons sifted cake flour
-or- 1 cup minus 2 tablespoons all-purpose flour (unsifted)
-or- 1 ½ cups breadcrumbs
-or- 1 cup all-purpose flour minus 2 tablespoons

<u>Self-rising flour, 1 cup</u>
1 cup all-purpose flour, 1 teaspoon baking powder plus ½ teaspoon salt

<u>Brown sugar, 1 cup packed</u>
1 cup granulated white sugar

<u>Granulated white sugar, 1 cup</u>
1 cup corn syrup (decrease liquid called for in recipe by 1/4 cup)
-or- 1 cup firmly packed brown sugar
-or- 1 cup honey (decrease liquid called for in recipe by 1/4 cup)

<u>Powdered confectioners sugar, 1 cup</u>
1 cup sugar plus 1 tablespoon cornstarch (processed in food processor)

Dairy Products

<u>Butter, ½ cup</u>
½ cup margarine (1 stick; do not substitute
whipped or low-fat margarine when baking)

<u>Egg</u>
1 large = 1/4 cup egg substitute = 2 egg yolks
2 large = 3 small eggs

-----Lagniappe----

Buttermilk, low-fat or fat-free, 1 cup
1 tablespoon vinegar or lemon juice plus low-fat or fat-free milk to make 1 cup (let stand 10 minutes)

Broth, beef or chicken

Canned broth, 1 cup
1 bouillon cube or 1 teaspoon bouillon granules dissolved in 1 cup boiling water
-or- 1 teaspoon Bouillon granules

Seasoning Products

Allspice, ground, 1 teaspoon
1/2 teaspoon ground cinnamon plus 1/2 teaspoon ground cloves

Bay leaf, 1 whole
1/4 teaspoon crushed bay leaf

Garlic, 1 small clove
1/8 teaspoon garlic powder or minced dried garlic

Herbs, fresh, chopped, 1 tablespoon
1 teaspoon dried herbs or 1/4 teaspoon ground herbs

Mustard, dried, 1 teaspoon
1 tablespoon prepared mustard

Parsley, dried, 1 teaspoon
1 tablespoon fresh parsley, chopped

Vegetables

<u>Onions, chopped, 1 medium</u>
1 tablespoon dried minced onion
1 teaspoon onion powder

<u>Peppers, red or green bell, chopped, 3 tablespoons</u>
1 tablespoon dried sweet red or green pepper flakes

Miscellaneous Products

<u>Vinegar, balsamic, 1/2 cup</u>
1/2 cup red wine vinegar (some flavor difference)

Index

C

CAKE

CANDY

CHICKEN

CHOCOLATE

COOKIES

CORN

D

DESSERTS

RICE

SALADS

SALSA

SAUCES

SEAFOOD

Notes to Myself

Take a moment to collect new recipes, make comments on favorites within Down Home Delicious, and note those that received rave reviews.

Date	Page #	Recipe	Comments

Notes to Myself

Take a moment to collect new recipes, make comments on favorites within Down Home Delicious, and note those that received rave reviews.

Date	Page #	Recipe	Comments

Notes to Myself

Take a moment to collect new recipes, make comments on favorites within Down Home Delicious, and note those that received rave reviews.

Date	Page #	Recipe	Comments

Notes to Myself

Take a moment to collect new recipes, make comments on favorites within Down Home Delicious, and note those that received rave reviews.

Date	Page #	Recipe	Comments

Down Home Delicious

Spice up your life with incredible Gulf Coast cooking by Peggy Touchtone Sholly

ORDERS MAY BE PLACED ONLINE AT

www.stonywood.com

Email: orders@stonywood.com

OR

Mail form to:

Stonywood Publications
P. O. Box 1590
Pearland, Texas 77581

FAX or Phone:

Fax: 281-482-8887
Phone: 832-215-3023
Toll-Free: 800-335-1280

Please place my order for _____ copies of *Down Home Delicious*
at the retail price of $27.95 per cookbook $ _____

Texas residents add 8.25% sales tax (*$2.30 per book*) $ _____

TOTAL: (COOKBOOK ORDER PLUS SALES TAX) $ _____

Postage and handling: (Cookbooks may be shipped directly to the address
listed below. Please add postage and handling for shipped delivery service.)

$6.00 for first book $ _____

$3.00 for each additional $ _____

TOTAL DUE AT TIME OF ORDER: $ _____

Please make checks payable to: Stonywood Publications

SHIP TO: Name (Business Name) _____

Address _____

City _____ ST _____ ZIP _____

Daytime Phone # _____ E-Mail (optional) _____

VISA _____ MasterCard _____ American Express _____

Account # _____ Exp. Date _____